APPLES
Are SQUARE

Dr Susan Smith Kuczmarski is a well-known expert on values-based leadership. For over three decades, she has conducted innovative leadership programs, taught at seven universities, worked in three non-profits, including the United Nations, and co-founded the innovation consulting firm, Kuczmarski & Associates. She currently teaches "Creating and Leading A Culture of Innovation" at Northwestern University's Kellogg School of Management. Trained as a cultural anthropologist, she has extensively researched how leadership skills are learned. A teacher of teachers for ten years and known for her innovative style, Dr Kuczmarski offers interactive seminars on leadership and culture for corporate, non-profit, and educational audiences.

Thomas D. Kuczmarski is co-founder and senior partner at Kuczmarski & Associates, a nationally recognized new products, services, and innovation management consulting firm. He has written four books on innovation, including *Innovating...Chicago-Style, Managing New Products, Innovation,* and *Innovating the Corporation*. In 2001, he co-founded the annual Chicago Innovation Awards. For over 30 years, he has been an adjunct professor at Northwestern University's Kellogg School of Management, where he teaches his popular executive courses on innovation. He was a brand manager at Quaker Oats and a principal at Booz, Allen & Hamilton.

APPLES Are SQUARE

Thinking Differently About Leadership

SUSAN SMITH KUCZMARSKI, ED.D.
AND THOMAS D. KUCZMARSKI

RUPA

Published by
Rupa Publications India Pvt. Ltd 2023
7/16, Ansari Road, Daryaganj
New Delhi 110002

Sales Centres:
Prayagraj Bengaluru Chennai
Hyderabad Jaipur Kathmandu
Kolkata Mumbai

Copyright © Susan Smith Kuczmarski and Thomas D. Kuczmarski 2023

Original English language edition published by Book Ends Publishing 2001 N. Halsted Street, Suite#201, Chicago Illinois 60164, USA. Arranged via Licensor's Agent: DropCap Inc

The views and opinions expressed in this book are the authors' own and the facts are as reported by them which have been verified to the extent possible, and the publishers are not in any way liable for the same.

All rights reserved.
No part of this publication may be reproduced, transmitted, or stored in a retrieval system, in any form or by any means, electronic, mechanical, photocopying, recording or otherwise, without the prior permission of the publisher.

P-ISBN: 978-93-5702-125-8
E-ISBN: 978-93-5702-126-5

First impression 2023

10 9 8 7 6 5 4 2 3 1

Printed in India

This book is sold subject to the condition that it shall not, by way of trade or otherwise, be lent, resold, hired out, or otherwise circulated, without the publisher's prior consent, in any form of binding or cover other than that in which it is published.

Contents

Foreword by Deepak Chopra xv

Introduction xvii

PART I: DEFINING THE CHARACTERISTICS OF SUCCESS

1. Apples Are Square   3
2. A New Success Model   13
3. Humility   25
4. Compassion   35
5. Transparency   53
6. Inclusiveness   67
7. Collaboration   83
8. Values-Based Decisiveness   97

PART II: ACTIVATING THE SEVEN STEPS TO CHANGE

9. Step 1—Reach Out to Serve Others   115
10. Step 2—Ask, "Who Am I?"   131
11. Step 3—Ask, "Who Are You?"   145
12. Step 4—Find Common Ground   157
13. Step 5—Don't Take the Pleats Out   173
14. Step 6—Root for People   187
15. Step 7—Leave Some Money on the Table   201
16. Lift People Up   215

Epilogue: The Peopleship Planet 225

About the Authors

In 1995, the authors collaborated to write their pioneering book, *Values-Based Leadership*, which launched the values in the workplace movement. Once again, they combine their expertise to boldly champion six innovative leadership qualities to kick off the next frontier.

Dr. Susan Smith Kuczmarski is a well-known expert on values-based leadership. For over three decades, she has conducted innovative leadership programs, taught at seven universities, worked in three non-profits, including the United Nations, and co-founded the innovation consulting firm, Kuczmarski & Associates. She currently teaches "Creating and Leading A Culture of Innovation" at Northwestern University's Kellogg School of Management. Trained as a cultural anthropologist, she has extensively researched how leadership skills are learned. A teacher of teachers for ten years and known for her innovative style, Dr. Kuczmarski offers interactive seminars on leadership and culture for corporate, non-profit, and educational audiences. The author of four award-winning books, she holds a Doctorate in Education and two master's degrees from Columbia University, where she was named an International Fellow, as well as a BA from Colorado College, where she returns every year to teach leadership. A lively radio and television guest, she has appeared on the *Today Show* and is widely quoted in print, including *Fast Company*, *The Wall Street Journal*, *Investor's Business Daily*, *CNN Money*, and *The Hindu*. She has been listed in *Who's Who in the World* for 12 years, and included in *Outstanding People of the 21st Century*, *500 Leaders of World Influence*, and *International Who's Who of Professional and Business Women*.

Thomas D. Kuczmarski is co-founder and senior partner at Kuczmarski & Associates, a nationally recognized new products, services, and innovation management consulting firm. He has written four books on innovation, including *Innovating...Chicago-Style*, *Managing New Products*, *Innovation*, and *Innovating the Corporation*. In 2001, he co-founded the annual Chicago Innovation Awards. For over 30 years, he has been an adjunct professor at Northwestern University's Kellogg School of Management, where he teaches his popular executive courses on innovation. He was a brand manager at Quaker Oats and a principal at Booz, Allen & Hamilton. He holds two master's degrees in business and international affairs from Columbia University, and a BA from the College of the Holy Cross. He is regularly quoted in the *Wall Street Journal, Fortune, Newsweek, Investor's Business Daily, USA Today, Advertising Age*, and the *Chicago Sun-Times*. He has appeared on the *Today Show*, and speaks on the topic of innovation around the world. His research, writing, books, speeches, seminars, teaching, and pragmatic consulting have made him one of the top leading experts in his field.

Married for three decades, the authors live in Chicago and are the parents of three adult sons.

To get information about consulting, teaching and speeches contact the authors at: *www.kuczmarski.com*.

Acknowledgments

This book has been a collaborative effort. First and foremost, we are deeply grateful to the 25 talented, inspirational, and energetic values-based leaders who we interviewed for this project. We have listed them on the next page. We would especially like to thank Dipak Jain, Dean of INSEAD, for his insight and wisdom in identifying the importance of values-based decisiveness, our sixth leadership quality.

The 25 leaders in *Apples Are Square* have continued to pioneer our new form of leadership since we first interviewed them in 2007. In this second edition, we would like to highlight some of their impressive accomplishments and progress in perpetuating values-based leadership.

Henry Givray, currently the Chairman, President & CEO of SmithBucklin, has continued to be a dedicated, ongoing student of leadership. He has been invited to speak at more than 50 engagements since 2007 and has articles published in *Business Week* and *Crain's Chicago Business*. In March 2011, Mr. Givray launched the SmithBucklin Leadership Learning Forum, an intensive 12-month program for a small group of top-performers who are exposed to leadership concepts, principles and guidelines in order to stimulate and inspire individual learning, self-discovery, and personal growth.

Charles Lewis has continued to be a strong innovative leader, having founded a new nonprofit organization, the Investigative Reporting Workshop in 2008, which is a center within the School of Communication at American University. Mr. Lewis became a full professor with tenure at American University in 2010. There are now 60 or more nonprofit news publishers nationwide since Mr. Lewis founded the Center for Public Integrity in 1989, the second in the U.S. He also co-founded the Investigative News Network in 2009. Finally, Mr. Lewis is completing his sixth book, tentatively titled *The Future of Truth: Power, the News Media and the Public's Right to Know* (PublicAffairs; 2013).

Carol Bernick currently serves as CEO of Polished Nickel Capital Management and as Chair-elect of Northwestern Memorial Healthcare. Until the acquisition of the Alberto Culver Company in May, 2011, she served as Executive Chairman of Alberto-Culver, a $1.6 billion global manufacturer of consumer products. Mrs. Bernick initiated and directed the process that led to the company's acquisition by Unilever.

Kimberly Senior has continued in the world of theater as an Artistic Associate at Next Theatre, Strawdog Theatre, and Chicago Dramatists. As an educator, Kimberly spent ten years as both an administrator and Resident Artist with Steppenwolf for Young Adults. In 2010, Ms. Senior received Columbia College's 2010 Excellence in Teaching Award.

Since retiring from Wisconsin Film and Bag in 2007, Jack Riopelle has pursued a "new career" of giving back to others. Leveraging his 41+ years in the business world, Mr. Riopelle is now the director of nine different Boards of Directors, mentors his pastor, two CEO's and three other senior executives on leadership, participates in speaking and consulting engagements, and has founded the "The Institute for Entrepreneurship and Innovation" affiliated with the University of Wisconsin – Green Bay.

Scott Lutz became CEO and President at Grocery Shopping Network, Inc. in 2010. This digital firm helps make shopping easier for grocery shoppers. In addition to hosting websites for thousands of grocery stores in the United States, the firm creates a shopper-relevant advertising network with a unique digital DNA that can be used to better market to shoppers.

Virginia L. Gilmore, Chairperson of the Board, Sophia Foundation, Inc., has focused her leadership efforts in nurturing the Sophia Foundation into a charitable organization that seeks to make a real difference in the world. The Sophia Foundation has the vision of "creating caring community" by fulfilling its mission to nurture the spirit, dignity and potential of people through transformative compassionate leadership.

Robin Gilman currently works as an associate of Arora Innovations, an executive consulting group, and as a scientific and communications consultant working at the Wrigley Global Innovation Center. Robin has also returned to the laboratory and is using his doctorate in bio-medical engineering to create new computer-based imaging technologies to support oral health research and other challenging chewing gum issues.

Leon Despres, legendary Chicago progressive alderman, passed away at the age of 101 on May 6, 2009. Despres was a champion of civil rights, one of the rare white aldermen in the 1950s and 1960s who sought to desegregate the city's neighborhoods, schools, and parks. His long, distinguished life should be an inspiration for leaders across the nation.

The Chicago City Day School made the decision a decade ago to hold fast to its conviction that a half-day developmental kindergarten program is optimal for young children. Galeta Kaar Clayton, the founder and headmistress of the school, believes that young children learn to interact with one another and make sense of their world through imaginary play. As a result, the Chicago City Day School launched a new program in September, 2011 called Play Day. A half-day voluntary program for five year-olds, Play Day affords children simple, unscheduled, independent "non-screen" time to be creative, to reflect, and to decompress. In short, to play. The program is child-driven—not adult-directed. The magic of this innovative program is that it is compatible with children's maturational levels, it is staffed by an early childhood teacher, and it leaves the half-day kindergarten class intact.

Finally, to our close group of friends and colleagues who are always there for us, personally and professional, including Bryan Brochu, Kevin Boehm, Tyler Comann, Diane Dahl, Martha Donovan, Colleen Dudgeon-Ransdell, Reven Fellars, Marina Gorey, Michael Krauss, James Kuczmarski, Dan and Michele Miller, Sally Parsons, Erica Regunberg, Gary Slack, and Christina Van Pelt. We extend a special thanks to our friend, Beth Ylvisaker, whose strength and spirit guides us in our work. In her words, "our life is a little while, but our love is ever long and deepening."

Once again we would like to thank all of our leaders who helped us shape this book:

Corporate, entrepreneurial, and business worlds:

Jack Riopelle, former chairman of Wisconsin Film & Bag

Carol Bernick, CEO of Polished Nickel Capital Management, and former Chairman, Alberto-Culver

Randy Larrimore, retired CEO of United Stationers

Henry Givray, chairman, president, and CEO of SmithBucklin

Dean Kamen, president of DEKA Research

Craig Newmark, founder of craigslist

Robin Gilman, scientific and communications consultant, Wrigley Global Innovation Center

Paulette Cole, CEO and creative director of ABC Home and ABC Home & Planet Foundation

Jerry Fisher, retired VP of Corporate R & D at Baxter Healthcare

Brian Sorge, VP of Client Solutions, Lambert & Associates

Scott Lutz, CEO and President, Grocery Shopping Network, Inc.

Academic world:

Dipak Jain, Dean of INSEAD

Galeta Kaar Clayton, founder and headmistress, Chicago City Day School

Nonprofit sector:

Christopher Zorich, former NFL football star and attorney

Kimberly Senior, theatre director and arts educator
Joel Hall, founder of the Joel Hall Dance Center
Virginia Duncan Gilmore, founder of the Sophia Foundation

Entertainment industry:
Susan Anton, Broadway star, actress, and recording artist

Public policy sector:
Charles Lewis, founder of Investigative Reporting Workshop at American University and Investigative News Network
Kaethe Morris Hoffer, private feminist lawyer and activist

Personal empowerment:
Kevin Melville Jennings, healer and counselor

Government sector:
Mary Ellen Weber, former NASA astronaut
Jan Schakowsky, U.S. Congresswoman
Leon Despres, former Chicago alderman (now deceased)
Vincent Patton, retired Master Chief Petty Officer of the Coast Guard

Foreword by Deepak Chopra

Great leaders are self-aware. They are also conscious. They embrace an expanded awareness, allowing them to understand that the infinite details of the world are inextricably interwoven.

Impactful leaders are conscious of what is going on as situations unfold. They are in synchronicity with their environment.

The skills that comprise good leadership are formed from awareness—a trait that can be learned. When you have mastered the basics of being a conscious leader, you will be able to answer three key awareness-related questions: How am I responding? How are "they" responding? And how are "we" responding? In analyzing the results of these questions, awareness of the group and its needs are addressed.

Before you step into a situation, then, you want to be as tuned in as possible by aligning you body, mind, and soul as completely as you can. The secret here is that body, mind, and soul want to be in alignment. You cannot force them—there is no such method as working to become aware. Instead, you allow.

Leaders learn how to get in touch with the inner most essence of their being. This goes way beyond the ego. It is being fearless and free. It is accepting criticism and accepting one's self. All relationships are a reflection of one's relationship with the self. It enables one to have great insights into relationships with others.

Leaders and followers co-create each other. They form an invisible, synergistic bond. Leaders exist to embody the values that followers thirst for, while followers exist to find the leader's vision from inside them.

The authors, Susan and Tom Kuczmarski, believe that success should be defined as a combination of empowering the self while at the same time serving others. This definition dispels the myth that leaders at the top need to control and compete to be effective. Contrary to the old model for success, which was derived from money, control, power and ego, they believe there is a new model for greatness. It involves their six critical values—humility, compassion, transparency, inclusiveness, collaboration, and values-based decisiveness.

This book reflects the fruits of thinking differently about leadership by re-evaluating a tangled hierarchy. It bursts with pride, both for what these new leaders have accomplished and for what is yet to come. It offers a new model of leadership that promotes fulfillment for the lives of leaders and their followers alike.

Enjoy these stories of twenty-five "square apples" and learn their secrets. You will discover a model of leadership necessary to move from an age of information to a culture that is knowledge-based, and ultimately, driven by wisdom. The future depends on the survival of the wisest and on leadership that is based on inner values.

All love,

Deepak Chopra

Introduction

The underlying assumptions of leadership have massively changed. The "control and compete" mindset has shifted. People are now seeking a more collaborative work environment rather than a competitive one. Consequently, leaders at the top of organizations need to modify their fundamental beliefs about the characteristics of good leadership.

Our book's vital message is: effective leaders serve others, who in turn leverage their inner strengths to accomplish great things. This message is beginning to spread around the world. It explains why *Apples Are Square* has received an enthusiastic response and has been printed in various languages, including editions in China, Taiwan, and South Korea.

There are three key elements involved. First, since the job of a leader is to now serve the people, a leader needs to find ways to view things from this new service-oriented perspective. This means, second, that leadership is not about pointing out other people's weaknesses and faults, but rather, about leveraging their strengths. For example, performance reviews should focus on accomplishments, key strengths, and growth goals for the future—not performance deficiencies. This requires a change from the typical emphasis on people's faults to focusing upon a new depth of understanding of people's capabilities. Third, the ultimate goal of leadership is to accomplish great things. This requires motivating people in ways that makes them feel valued and recognizing that their contributions count toward achieving a common set of goals.

To accomplish these new people-sensitive goals, today's leader must explore one's self to discover his or her inner motivations. More than ever before, understanding, recognizing, and articulating individual values is a key starting point for effective leadership. Importantly, individual values help identify the collective values of an organization. When values are out of sync with norms and behaviors, a rift begins to form, causing people to feel disconnected from their organization.

We are thrilled to have Deepak Chopra write the Foreword to this second edition of *Apples Are Square*. He strongly believes that self-reflection and self-consciousness serve as the driving force behind strong leaders. He also believes in our six key values, which we propose are the innovative cornerstones for successful leaders in the future. These include humility, compassion, transparency, inclusiveness, collaboration, and values-based decisiveness. Together, these six unique qualities define the new core of leadership.

Since 1995, when we published out first leadership book, *Values-Based Leadership*, we have seen the field of leadership undergo a gigantic transformation. The archetypal "old boy" leader found at the top of government, academia, and business organizations is shifting to a diverse, younger, and more open style of leader. We are optimistic for the future as more and more leaders understand that their role is to share leadership, relinquish control, collaborate, and focus on serving others rather than one's self. We believe that this new team-oriented leader, our "square apple," can play the game differently, innovatively, and effectively.

Each of our six leadership qualities, described in this book, serves to motivate groups, inspire individuals, and fortify organizations to accomplish great things. When you read each of our compelling examples of leadership, we know that you will experience the same energy that we did. Undeniably, the voices of our "square apples" will strike a chord in many hearts. Reshaping a bad apple or work environment is not easy. Yet, in our hands, we hold the ability to create a more dynamic, inclusive, and collaborative organization. We hope you will feel charged to master the six essential values of new leadership, communicate in innovative ways that inspire people to serve others, and build strong relationships for a sense of community.

Susan and Tom Kuczmarski

I

Defining
—THE—
Characteristics
of Success

1

Apples Are Square

"We must always change, renew, rejuvenate ourselves; otherwise we harden."
GOETHE

SO, WHY SQUARE FRUIT?

"Value the small voice inside that tells us to do the right thing," says Christopher Zorich, a former defensive linemen for the Chicago Bears and the Washington Redskins. At the height of his professional football career, when he was making millions of dollars, what did he spend his money on? Lots of bling? Fast cars? Faster women? Mansions? Other kinds of conspicuous consumption? No, he established The Christopher Zorich Foundation in honor of his mother. The purpose of the foundation is to feed and help needy neighborhood children and their families. Then, when his football days ended, he went back to school to earn his law degree to help manage the affairs of the foundation.

Our book title was taken from this inspiring anecdote. Chris reflects on his boyhood years:

> "My mom had to go through some rough circumstances, but she always kept a positive attitude. We never had a motto in the house or anything. I learned by watching her and seeing

how she was able to turn a negative into a positive. Sometimes we didn't have food in the house, so we would either not eat that evening, or we would go to the local supermarket. It closed at 9:30 PM. We'd search through the dumpsters for food, and look for rotten apples and stuff like that. We kind of made a joke about it sometimes, but I didn't know apples were round until I was older. I thought all apples were square because my mom would take a knife and cut or square off the bad spots. Then, we would sit and eat our squared apples."

Zorich's life certainly reflects lessons from his mother. No pithy sayings, no clever mottos, no bumper sticker morality. He lives his and his mother's values through his actions.

"Squared apples" symbolically stand for a new way to lead in the workplace and a new way to measure success—both personally and professionally. While Chris Zorich's mother took rotten apples and literally reshaped them into something edible and appealing, we, as a society, need to take bruised work environments and reshape them into dynamic, inclusive, and collaborative organizations.

Likewise, we need to re-examine the central core within our own personal life. Is the core selfish or selfless? Is our primary motivation to achieve material gains for ourselves and control the people around us? Is our orientation geared towards using people or getting the most out of them for themselves as well as for the good of the organization? Serving others, helping others, and inspiring others to bring out their inner core of strengths and talents is what the new definition of success is all about.

THE NEED TO CHANGE

During the next 25 years, organizations will have to undergo revolutionary change. There is a critical need for a fundamental shift in leadership, driven by an equally critical need for imaginative thinking about the meaning of success. In the workplace of the past, leaders tended to be authoritarian, aggrandizing, and arrogant. Future leaders will need to communicate in ways that inspire others to learn more about themselves and serve others. Does this sound too good to be true? Not really—the world truly needs to change. Tomorrow's leaders need to be engaging, unpretentious, and even compassionate and self-effacing. *Apples Are Square* tells us how to begin. We must bring a new vision, belief structure, and focus to the workplace, our families, and our own personal lives because too many contemporary organizations are dysfunctional and ill-equipped to cope with the challenges of the future. We need a new model—a new leadership style and success formula—that we describe in our last chapter as "peopleship." This new archetype emphasizes the people within an organization rather than the leader. As an economist might phrase it, an organization will endure if its culture "bubbles up" from the employees rather than "trickles down" from the leaders at the top.

THE OLD SUCCESS FORMULA

Size defined success in the 1990s. How big was your bonus? How large was your portfolio? How many options did you have? What was your net worth? What was the market value of your company? Americans in the business world were seeking a way to get rich quickly in order to retire early. The ability to accumulate wealth and plan for retirement determined self-worth. Success was defined financially, not by the contribution you made to the people around you or to the world you inhabited.

The strength of this self-centered standard for success began to dissolve at the beginning of the 21st century. The economy flattened; the stock market crashed; many people lost their jobs; global terrorism reigned; pension funds collapsed; and the dreams of wealth and early retirement—the 90s benchmark for success—seemed like vague memories from a distant time. The greed that seemed to take over as a core value for many leaders has gotten them into trouble. The list of fallen leaders is embarrassingly long and lengthens every day. Take a look at the following corporate, political, religious, and sports figures that have made infamous appearances in recent headlines:

- Bernard Ebbers of WorldCom
- Richard Scrushy of Healthsouth
- Cardinal Bernard Law of the Boston Archdiocese
- Jose Conseco of Major League Baseball
- Dennis Kozlowski of Tyco International
- Hank Greenberg of AIG
- Jeffrey Skilling of Enron
- John Rigas of Adelphia Communications
- Harry Stonecipher and Phil Condet of Boeing
- The Honorable Tom Delay of the U.S. House of Representatives

What do these leaders all have in common? They share an outdated and archaic style of leadership.

They represent the "old guard": egocentric leaders who embraced a "control and compete" mind-set. They focused on *their* needs rather than the needs of their people. They did not deliver as promised, committed serious ethical errors, lacked a solid set of values, and incurred both mistrust and disdain. They also cost their organizations dearly in terms of prestige, reputation, and financial well-being. In some cases, they even destroyed their organizations as well as those that relied upon them.

NORMLESSNESS HAS COME TO ROOST

Our pioneering 1995 book, *Values-Based Leadership* (Prentice Hall), predicted this problem. It discussed how the culture of the workplace could not remain productive without a shared set of values and norms that would join employees and management together. Now, 12 years later, this "normlessness" has come to permeate business, government, and even sports. CEOs are knocked down by scandals and improprieties; politicians exchange morality for votes; and professional athletes are tarnished by the use of steroids. We need a new way of doing business and a new model of leadership. Most of all, we clearly need to place far more attention on people, the most valuable "assets" and essence of any organization.

As leaders, we can choose to do business differently and still make profits. Jim Sinegal, the CEO of Costco Wholesale, the nation's fifth largest retailer, leads with a different set of values. On average, Costco workers are considerably better compensated than their competitors, but good wages and benefits have contributed to low employee turnover. Jim states, "This approach is good business." He is absolutely right. Bill Gates is another leader who does not fit the same outdated mold—and he sure hasn't done too badly either.

We present a new model of leadership that is based upon leaders serving their constituents rather than the other way around. In so doing, a leader's role is to foster a culture shaped by values and norms that helps maximize the potential and power of individuals within organizations. This new model cultivates multiple leaders, empowers individuals, enables them to be recognized and valued, and connects employees and managers by building strong relationships.

This "people business" is the next management frontier. We have all been through "quick-hit" management fads and programs—from reengineering to rightsizing to outsourcing. Today, however, loyalty is dead. Employees do not feel valued or secure; they feel overworked, overstretched, and overburdened. Rampant cost-cutting and downsizing continue to be viewed as "preferred" methods for increasing earnings. Most people predict this situation will only get worse. Some call it the "new normal"; others more accurately call it "dysfunctional."

Our new leadership archetype offers a prescription—a new proposition—for organizations to change their culture as their leaders rebuild, rekindle trust, and renew faith in the workplace. It will inspire a new sense of personal hope by changing the way leaders behave, communicate, and energize people. Most importantly, it will infuse a new set of values and norms into organizations. As our new model of leadership encourages personal risk-taking, creativity, and flexibility, companies, in particular, will be better able to gain a competitive edge. As organizations and their leaders take time to figure out their new form of leadership, the ones that adopt a new mind-set more quickly will emerge ahead of the pack.

Meg Whitman, CEO of eBay, exemplifies this new leadership archetype. Rather than the old-guard, command-and-control environment, she has strived to build a values-based community that integrates and links her customers to her employees. She believes in giving control to the community of users. Meg says: "we enable, not direct or mandate. We partner with our customers and let them and our employees take the company where they think it is best utilized. It's a partnership."

Procter & Gamble, under the leadership of A.G. Lafley, is a great example of a company that has reached out to developers, beyond the internal R & D staff. Lafley believes that forming outside "partnerships" with suppliers, vendors, and customers enables greater innovation to occur. He also believes strongly in listening to consumers on a frequent basis. By uncovering their problems, his company is able to create new products that solve them.

Even in companies where the often random and elusive stock market forces leaders to make rash decisions, our approach of lifting people up can work. It can empower a workforce, link it more closely to its customers, increase earnings, and boost morale.

SUCCESS—GIVING VERSUS TAKING

Chris Zorich created a radically different model of success. He used his fame and fortune to build something he thought was bigger and better. What really happened to him, however, was something deeper and not so obvious. He listened to the small voice inside. He experienced an inner wisdom and wanted to share who he was at his core. Chris created a plan that connected him to a more meaningful career and in so doing started The Christopher Zorich Foundation aimed at helping the homeless. "I just had this burning desire to hopefully affect change on a larger scale," he says.

At the same time, it is still perfectly fine to make money, generate profits, and acquire assets. The key is the way that goals are reached and the value placed on them. Many average-income workers donate time, focus on giving to children and families, and help their communities. It's not about making money; it's about figuring out how best to make a positive impact. Of course, sometimes lots of money can be used for the good of mankind. Bill Gates and Warren Buffet, two billionaires, have decided to give back. Buffet is donating $41 billion to the Gates Foundation. Their combined $70 billion in assets will make quite a mark on world poverty, health care, and education throughout the globe.

In contrast, greed has prevailed within many corporate cultures. Gordon ("Greed is good!") Gekko, a character from the 1987 movie *Wall Street*, was a case of art imitating life. Success is all about stock price and earnings increases—not about doing what is right for the customers, employees, and shareholders. CEO compensation seems to grow every year. Yet the millions of dollars in salary that CEOs receive still have little to do with how the company performs.

Furthermore, as individuals we seem to measure our progress more and more by how well we are doing financially rather than what we are doing and why. We can hardly imagine a community of people who focus on helping and serving others and providing for the good of the community after their personal needs are fulfilled.

In short, square apples involve changing not only our leadership approach but our organizational culture as well, and changing how we measure success. Individually, we need to adopt a "servant mind-set" and balance more of our needs with the needs of others. In so doing, we hope to cut off the rotten parts in order to avoid further decay.

REDEFINING SUCCESS

How do you define success? What's most important to you in your life? Is it a happy marriage, good friends, loving children, a satisfying job, meaningful contributions, or financial independence?

How does the organization you work for define success? Is it ever-increasing profits, higher stock prices, greater employee productivity, lower costs, or higher investment returns?

You can see the gap that exists: a disparity between employee happiness and management needs. Leaders have not traditionally focused on the human side of leadership. While organizations sell products, serve members, and provide services, they tend to neglect their most important asset: the people who work there. And yet, it is these people who get results within organizations. The "human advantage" is the best competitive advantage that a company or organization could ever have—but rarely is it viewed that way.

We need a new metric for success and a new leadership paradigm that positively impacts every employee and manager within any organization, while at the same time ensuring the success of the organization itself. This new metric will merge and enhance employee welfare, dignity, and happiness, instead of placing them in opposition.

The payoff of this new leadership construct will be a highly functioning organization that succeeds at every level, including increased profitability and better satisfaction of customer needs. That is the whole point. We can take a new people-oriented approach to leadership and still drive up stock price or build membership and value. The two are not only compatible, but mutually beneficial.

A NEW WAY OF LEADERSHIP

Hank Greenberg, the former CEO of AIG who is currently under federal investigation, recently claimed: "A new world order of heightened scrutiny has arrived. We need to get tougher, demand more, and expect greater results from employees. CEOs need to take charge. The world has changed." He is right. The world has changed, but not in the way he implies. He believes that we need more authoritarian-based, self-centered, and self-promoting leadership. Nothing could be further from the truth. The changed world of the 21st century has a dire need for a new kind of leader and a new form of leadership—a new model—with the sensibilities to meet the challenges in our social, business, and personal lives.

Here is the key point: Greenberg's model of success did not include people in the definition of organizational success. He missed the idea that people's lives are holistic and require a balance of job, family, community, and self. Recognizing and respecting this balance is lost within many companies and organizations today.

Our need for change requires a new archetype. The old management approach was to roll with the punches—don't express yourself emotionally because it meant you were weak. Distance yourself—be arrogant! The new leadership paradigm asks you to contribute your total self, express yourself emotionally, and show that you care. Add texture to your relationships so that employees and managers link and bond. Show personal warmth, pulling others in by listening and asking questions. This type of emotional communication builds a culture of caring within the organization. If leadership has this emotional depth, then their organizations can perpetuate a new enabling culture.

Many large contemporary organizations lack energy, passion, and loyalty. However, organizations can structure themselves and create a mind-set to provide a bridge to connect everyone through an effective shared leadership construct. The key ingredients of this new leadership mind-set are our six core qualities and the seven steps to change. We are confident that each of these new leadership qualities can demonstrably change the workplace and alter how we ultimately view success and failure.

Our 25 interviewees gave us thought-provoking and stirring responses. There were no canned answers. They shared candid and vulnerable insights on their inner lives, thinking processes, and personal values. We were moved, inspired, and energized by their thoughts on leadership. Each of the leaders interviewed was a pioneer in his or her field. As a result of their perspectives and personal definitions of success, a new meaning of leadership emerges. It involves a genuine interest in and caring for others, developing their qualities, and treating them with respect. The workplace becomes more like an engaged and supportive community, than a "work hard and get paid" treadmill. We now strongly accept as true that the new business frontier is just this—a caring group. Kindness, mutual respect, and passion are present. Differences are accepted and, in fact, nurtured. Not only does an employee's growth and development receive focus, but the quality of their relationship with other employees also becomes a paramount concern. It is no surprise, then, that loyalty returns. We believe this emphasis on people will become mainstream.

This new workplace is a helping community, in which each member of a small nurturing group supports and calls out one another's genius by making themselves present and available in the group. The sense of empathy in a helping community encourages individuals to reach their maximum potential by having members nourish and elicit each other's strengths. It *is* like a family, a community, a closely knit team of people with mutual goals and vision.

Employees have the capacity to pursue individual growth and apply their own desires, enthusiasm, and skills to the workplace. This allows an individual to work at his or her optimal capacity, and have the freedom and creative fire to impassion the workplace.

Jack Riopelle, CEO of Wisconsin Film & Bag, suggests that a shift is to come: "I think most leaders need to exhibit the humanness inside them . . . that they are human, and that, at times, they are frightened to death. We are all on uncharted waters right now. I think employees need to see passion and compassion. I think employees need to see exhilaration. I think employees need to see laughter. I think employees need to see tears. I think employees need to see the humanness of the leader. And a lot of leaders have a very difficult time doing that. They put themselves in a box. They've got a three-foot shield around themselves. And they're not perceived as human. And I don't think that's a good thing." All 25 "square apples" would surely agree.

2

A New Success Model

"Be not afraid of growing slowly; be afraid only of standing still."
CHINESE PROVERB

THE NEW SUCCESS METRICS

Are you successful? How do you define success for yourself? Regardless of how you answer, the response lies within these questions: Do you improve the lives of other people? Do you make them feel better about themselves? Do you make them feel like they are capable of achieving more than they ever thought they could? The new paradigm for success places more emphasis on the individual or the people within the organization, whether the setting is profit or nonprofit.

Success is not about power, wealth accumulation, and hierarchical control. Success should be about two things—how one feels about one's self (self-esteem, self-confidence, and self-perception) and the impact that one has at home, at work, and in the community.

There is a new kind of energy when people-based leaders run the show. Jerry Fisher, former senior vice president at Baxter believes that, "leaders have to have passion, they have to be an energy source, they have to listen, they have to be simplifiers, they have to filter the noise, they have to bring the picture into focus, and they have to be decisive on simple and tough issues. They have to genuinely care. And I think they need to be predictable. If my people are surprised, I have left something out somewhere."

He is thinking and acting quite differently than Hank Greenberg! Jerry believes that a successful leader infuses energy, builds confidence, and stimulates co-workers. When this leader walks away, employees feels exhilarated, not depleted or defeated. Consequently, they will make more important contributions because they see their interests as the same as the organization that employs them.

• •

Making a Difference

Christopher Zorich
Former NFL football star and attorney

Football was Chris Zorich's ticket out of the impoverished neighborhood on the south side of Chicago that he called home as a child. It was his ticket to an education that he otherwise could never have afforded. It was his ticket to more money in one season of professional football than his mother had seen in 18 years on public aid.

Zorich cashed in his ticket, but he spent the proceeds on feeding others, not his ego. He used the financial payoff from his football career for others because the fame, the riches, and the comforts would never be enough. Making an impact once a week for a few months a year did not satisfy Zorich. Instead, he focused on making a difference for the people he knew best: the poor, hungry, neglected children of his former hometown.

He established The Christopher Zorich Foundation in 1993 to honor his mother, who died during his senior year of college. The organization provides educational programs for Chicago-area youth, delivers groceries during the holidays to needy families, and brings flowers to mothers in shelters. Over the past decade, the foundation has touched the lives of more than 100,000 individuals, enough people to fill several football stadiums.

Zora Zorich, Chris's mother, did not fit the typical mold of a great leader. She spent her adult life on welfare, collecting $250 a month. However, her son never saw her cry and cannot remember a time when she was visibly upset. Mrs. Zorich would scavenge for fruit and candy for her son, only to share the small bounty with other hungry neighborhood children. She taught him how to play baseball and football. They were happy together.

"Being involved in sports, there are a lot of motivational things relating to success and winning," Zorich remembers. "I learned a lot from Coach (Lou) Holtz when I was playing football at the University of Notre Dame. He has this motto called WIN, which is an acronym for 'What's Important Now.' That applies as much to practicing tackling on Monday to be great in the game Saturday as it does to my mother focusing on where she would get our next meal. My mother wasn't as sophisticated at developing a motto but she certainly applied that winning philosophy."

Great leaders are not handed success; it is something they achieve in spite of their circumstances.

• •

Living Up to Your Standards

To lead with values requires the individual to develop a standard or perspective from which to judge what is right. It must be a self-initiated standard that creates consistency for an individual and can always be called upon. For Zorich, all he has to do is think about the woman who provided him with so many lessons.

"I don't want to sound like I am four years old, but I have this thing in the back of my mind that says, 'Would my mom be proud if X happened? Or if I did this would my mom be proud?'" Zorich says. "I have this fear that I am not going to take advantage of all the opportunities that are presented to me. I have been given a tremendous opportunity, and I need to take that and show other people that are in the circumstances I was in that they can succeed; I have this fear that all my mom lived for, all that I worked so hard for, will mean absolutely nothing. People say, 'Chris, you have already accomplished so much in your life,' but I still feel there is so much out there that needs to be done. I want to affect change on a major scale and, if I just take the easy way out, take a nice paying job in order to live comfortably; I would feel as though I let thousands and thousands of people down."

Chris's mother gave him the standard of helping others to the best of her ability. It is this same standard that has guided Chris to be the great values-based leader that he is today.

Finding Your Type of Success

Success is not a plaque or a dollar sign. It can't be bought or ascribed. Success is a personal reward borne out of a subscription to one's core values. For a business to be successful, the company and the individuals that comprise it must be committed to the same values. This unifies the goals of the organization by creating a standardized measure of success. Otherwise, everyone will pursue a different idea of success.

When Zorich established his foundation, it was not because he did not enjoy the game of football or that it didn't compensate him well. He walked away because his athletic accomplishments were not enough to fulfill his values. It would not be the right choice for everyone; it was the right choice for him because it allowed him to become "successful" by fulfilling his core values.

Working on What You Know

"What I want to do is instill in folks, young and/or old, that they can succeed," Zorich says. "Selfishly for me, I have created programs that I know about. I know about not having food in the house. I know about not being able to afford to go to school. I know about not having opportunities to go beyond the four blocks where I lived. I am looking to create an environment that fosters a sense of building the whole person—mind, body and spirit—versus not having a chance."

Having been in similar circumstances only years ago, Zorich had no trouble empathizing with the children on the south side of Chicago. However, empathy is a passive trait. What Zorich exhibits goes beyond empathy and demonstrates a form of compassion. What his foundation contributes makes an active and significant impact on people's lives.

Zorich explains, "My mom died of complications from diabetes. When I was playing football, a lot of people would say, 'Chris, your mom had diabetes, why don't you participate in the Juvenile Diabetes Fund?' Now that is a wonderful organization, but there are some issues around my block that I need to address like homelessness and lack of food. I knew more about those issues. Sure, I would help my mom with her treatments, but I am not a doctor so I am not sure what I could do aside from raise money for research. It is an important issue but I am limited in how I can affect change. I can feel and touch the folks we have assisted with my foundation. These issues are near and dear to my heart because I know what it is like as a child to have your stomach growling after lunch at school, or to go home and have nothing to eat."

Opening the Door to Others

In a typical hierarchical business structure, there is a lot of distance between those at the top and individuals at the bottom. The distance breeds unfamiliarity, distrust, and a mutual lack of respect. It is hard to know what people think if you never see their faces or hear their voices.

"I think leaders need to spend time dealing with folks that normally they wouldn't spend time with," Zorich shares. "When you are able to build a team, everyone is important. The CEO is just as important as the guy at the gate and if the CEO walks in the door and doesn't respect the guy at the gate, what kind of leader is he or she? Do they care about the people or do they care more about the company?"

Distance occurs not only when you insulate yourself from people you view as beneath you, but also when you shun people who are dissimilar to you. As Zorich affirms, "I think we need to move away from the traditional archetype of a leader and learn from groups of people that have been ignored in the past. Obviously I am talking about people of color or people of different sexual orientation that sometimes don't get figured into the 'All-American Pie.' When we think of All-American we think of blond hair, blue eyes, out in the suburbs. We need to transform what that look can be, and understand that there can be a diversity of experiences, and a diversity of ideas in the workplace."

SIX SIDES OF A SQUARED APPLE

The leader of the future will have to embrace six unique qualities that are unknown to most leaders today. Once the apple is "squared"—cut on the four sides as well as the top and the bottom—a six-sided apple will result. These can be seen as the six unique qualities that define the new core of leadership.

Our six new leadership qualities are: humility, compassion, transparency, inclusiveness, collaboration, and values-based decisiveness. Together, they form a new definition of success. In effect, they represent the new core. Emerging from our talks with leaders, this set of characteristics serves as the new leadership paradigm. Each quality is difficult to find in today's workplace. In fact, many leaders take little interest in them.

The six qualities are briefly introduced below. Each is discussed in detail in subsequent chapters.

Humility

Having humility means viewing oneself as insignificant. Self-perceptions of insignificance allow persons to let their egos go, and care more about listening to other points of view than about being right. Virginia Gilmore, founder of the Sophia Foundation, describes humility this way: "It has to do with caring about the relationship—the sacred connection—rather than your own power base. Humility is not always having the answer, but being the person who steps aside and lets the other person step out in front of you.

It's being able to do that dance—back and forth—to be able to learn, not know all of the answers, and be okay with that." While it's hard to pull this off, humility is our number-one leadership quality. Without this one in place, the others just won't be able to be nurtured.

Compassion

Compassion is all about having concern for the well-being of others—in effect, to suffer with them. It means understanding another person to such a degree that you can empathize entirely with their feelings and thoughts. It's more than just having empathy (the thought), however. One must do something with it (the action). Compassion means to be in the heart of another person. The closer we are to others, the more we can feel or relate to their situation—or be in their heart—and experience their emotions, whether confusion, pain, sorrow, misery, or happiness. A leader who is compassionate is gracious, generous, kind, supportive, and nonjudgmental.

Transparency

It is hard to have an honest dialogue with someone without the clarity that comes from knowing where they stand, even what they think and feel. Transparency means opening one's self up, being mentally and emotionally accessible to others, and yet still in touch with one's own self and needs. A transparent person is one who enables his thoughts and deeds to show through. This leadership trait is often seen as one that breeds weakness or vulnerability. Of course, transparency can make someone feel vulnerable, but it also makes a person feel more real, more genuine. Transparent organizations have fewer hidden agendas, and less time is spent trying to figure out their programs and plans. When transparency is in place, openness, fairness, integrity, and truthfulness permeate a relationship or organization.

Inclusiveness

Inclusiveness means to accept and recognize people's differences, relish their opinions and perspectives, and establish an environment where people are listened to, trusted, and valued. Hierarchy spoils a sense of inclusiveness. Inclusiveness requires leaders to get to know all their employees on a personal basis. "How is that possible if there are 500 people in my division," a leader might ask. Better get started today is how we strongly feel. You can't begin to make people feel included if you don't even know them. Inclusiveness means finding ways to connect with people and managing tasks and job responsibilities to ensure that the team is valued and rewarded. Most corporate compensation programs are based on individual accomplishment and the overall growth of the company or organization. By placing greater emphasis on the team, as a unit of recognition and compensation, *connection* among employees occurs. A newfound sense of togetherness brings strong feelings of inclusiveness.

Collaboration

Collaboration means partnership. It is all about working together to achieve a common goal. It means leveraging people's strengths and talents in a way that yields a far greater result than individuals trying to accomplish the same single-handedly. When we work with people, it has to be a win-win situation for everyone. Collaboration involves compromise. Without it, collaboration is just a word. Through compromise, a midpoint is reached where collaboration can occur. A series of personal "IOUs" can be built up over time between two people. As favors are done for one person, it helps to ensure that favors in the future will be returned. Oddly, there is often a sense of entitlement within many cultures. Employees don't want to collaborate if they have to do something that doesn't suit them. Similarly, leaders just assume that because employees are getting a paycheck they should perform their every command. While commonplace, this thinking has *no* collaborative quality to it!

Values-Based Decisiveness

Decisiveness means choosing a course of action or mental direction based on weighing several alternatives and considerations. Because we never actually see a decision, we know a decision has been made when other things start to happen. Decision making is integral to leadership. Important decisions have short- and long-term consequences for groups and communities. While the capacity for decision making is a necessary attribute for a leader, individual style varies. However when values guide the process, deciding on a course of action is trouble-free and effortless. The message is clear: values serve as a decision-making compass.

LIFT PEOPLE UP

Looking ahead, our 21st-century organization must undergo a seven-step, culture-altering revolutionary change. The seven steps are:

1. Reach out to serve others.
2. Ask, "Who am I?"
3. Ask, "Who Are You?"
4. Find common ground.
5. Don't take the pleats out.
6. Root for people.
7. Leave some money on the table.

Each of these steps becomes a distinct chapter and is discussed in detail in the second half of the book.

We believe there is a new way of doing business, and a new way to harness trust in *people*. Without question, people are any organization's source of energy, creativity, and emotional vibrancy. Any person in any organization can learn our innovative recipe for leadership.

Our leadership model is both practical and visionary. You will see that the process of trusting and working with people is as important, if not more important, as the process of making money. The new bottom line involves investing in the inner resources of workers, their personal growth and professional development, and creating a work culture and environment where leaders have a new way of treating people.

The 21st century will be marked by organizations trying to improve results through people, especially creative, energized people. Having the best people and getting their very best thinking and collaboration can profoundly impact organizations. People, no doubt, can completely alter the landscape of the workplace.

Imagine eliminating a tiered, layered organization. Employees and leaders end up working together more as equals—as partners. For sure, each will bring different skills, forms of intelligence, and contributions to the organization "party," but no one will feel like a subordinate *underneath* someone else in the organization. Future organizations will readily recognize the positive energy and effectiveness of creating a new model of leadership.

THE NEED FOR A NEW MIND-SET

We share a fervent belief that the future depends on a new mind-set. The impact of bringing our six qualities or the six sides of the squared apple—humility, compassion, transparency, inclusiveness, collaboration, and values-based decisiveness—to organizations can change the face and inner fiber of our workplace. Without them, many organizations will never reach their collective potential. Without them, many other organizations will simply fail. Our six qualities can serve as the needle and thread to strengthen the fabric and give new shape to the employee and workplace.

The first three qualities—humility, compassion, and transparency—are qualities that can be manifested individually without involvement from others. They are intrinsic, self-driven qualities. Other people activate the other three qualities—inclusiveness, collaboration, and decisiveness. You cannot collaborate by yourself; one needs to do that with others. Similarly, you cannot be inclusive or decisive within a group unless you are considering the needs of others and interacting with them.

Only through the infusion of these new qualities into organizations can we hope to once again restore their strength and vitality. It is our personal mission to help make organizations a better place to work and a more empowering environment for individual employees and leaders. If we achieve this, the writing of this book will be well worth it.

Let's take a closer look in the next few chapters at our new paradigm and its six qualities. We are optimistic that the current "drought" of effective leaders can be turned around, as leaders can easily learn them. Taken together, our "square apples" will reshape the *core* of success.

3

Humility

> *"A man wrapped up in himself makes a very small bundle."*
> BENJAMIN FRANKLIN

> *"Humility, like darkness, reveals the heavenly lights."*
> HENRY DAVID THOREAU

Before her mission to the International Space Station, astronaut Mary Ellen Weber traveled to the Kennedy Space Center with her crew to review the shuttle hardware, a standard prelaunch procedure. Before the review, Weber's mission commander gathered everyone just outside the space shuttle to share a story about a mistake he had made at such a review years ago in order to help this crew avoid similar mistakes. Weber recalls that this was a striking move in the often strict, no-mistakes-tolerated atmosphere of NASA, and particularly so, because this commander was one of the most highly revered in the astronaut corps for his performance and for his knowledge of shuttle systems. Indeed, by speaking so openly, not only did the commander enhance the crew's respect for him immeasurably, he set the precedent for humility on the ground and in space: everyone should avoid slipups, but if anyone falters, he or she should speak up about it, just as he had done right then and there. From that point on, members of the crew were not afraid to ask for help, which, in turn, produced a less stressful and more trusting and self-assuring atmosphere aboard the space shuttle, explains Weber. "I think if he did not convey his humility, our mission would not have been nearly as successful," she says. "We were not afraid to make mistakes. Nobody was ever afraid to admit that they did not know something or that they needed help. It was a really, really productive environment—not just for us but for the whole mission control."

Weber's story is anything but a special case. In a business environment, few things are more empowering than people like her commander who encourage open and honest communication. Weber's crew learned best by making mistakes. This method is true for almost every task in the workplace, whether it is making decisions, writing reports, giving presentations, conducting meetings, or leading project teams. Whether rocket scientists or computer analysts, people simply learn best by faltering first. Creating an environment in which such faltering feels okay is an imperative task. Business leaders need to support taking risks, encourage falling down, and then demonstrate how, exactly, to learn from false steps. If humility is absent, however, few will take risks in the first place.

WHAT IS HUMILITY?

The word *humility* is derived from the Latin term *humilitas*, meaning "insignificance." Such a word origin may strike the reader as odd—in the conventional sense, an insignificant person is perceived as having little value, a perception at odds with our statement that a humble leader has value in both professional and personal contexts. Within the framework of humility, however, "insignificance" explains a person accepting a diminished perception of him or her self. Accordingly, having humility means viewing one's self as insignificant.

Why would anyone want to view him or her self as insignificant? Awareness of our insignificance allows us to let our egos go and emphasize other points of view. In this sense, humility means learning not to be the one who always has the answer—but to be the one who steps aside and lets others provide answers of their own.

WHAT IS THE BENEFIT OF HUMILITY?

A myth pervades many business settings: employees should be intracompetitive in order to create an efficient workforce. They should beat the opposition, make the most money, and secure the most fame. The myth also stipulates that only the most competitive winners come out on top—that each person's success lowers the chances of someone else's. Our interviewees reveal, however, that such cutthroat competition creates a positively unbearable work environment.

A much happier, more productive work environment is one that emphasizes teamwork and achieving goals as a group, rather than as celebrity-conscious, status-seeking individuals. Yet if people are going to allow group goals to hold such importance, they must also have a substantial degree of humility—if they are prima donnas who do not play well with others, they can upset the energy of those around them and ruin the group dynamic, altogether.

Leaders need to adopt a humble, respectful outlook as well as care for the needs of everyone in their group. Take a second to consider why this is so important. When you really know that someone humble and respectful cares about you—whether it is personal or professional care—you respond and behave differently to that person. Typically, you are more unguarded, trusting, and secure. You are motivated and productive. This environment allows for more open and direct dialogue and communications, limits greatly any feeling of alienation, and helps to build trust in employee-to-employee or employee-to-executive relationships. Understandably, this caring attitude often distinguishes effective groups from dysfunctional ones.

How do we "do" caring? It starts by developing a caring attitude. Ask people personal questions that convey genuine interest. Help someone address a problem or issue with a concrete plan of steps. Listen to and gauge interest in someone's point of view. Talk to someone about the potential you see in him or her. Never be afraid to enter someone's "personal zone." You have to get involved with someone if you are talking to him or her about his or her inner strengths. Too often, people have been conditioned in organizations to avoid getting too personal. It is inappropriate to discuss certain topics, but it is appropriate to discuss inner talents and strengths that should and could be leveraged at work. Empower others to develop their own uniquely individual gifts. In addition, do not mandate reciprocity or expect "benefits" back in return. A caring attitude conveys a desire to give to others, to be considerate, and to convey genuine interest—all the time.

Dipak Jain believes the key to "doing" caring is to view others as working with you and not for you. When leaders or executives lack humility or consider themselves above other employees, they create inherent conflict within the organization. They limit resources available, and in doing so, limit the amount that the team as a whole is able to achieve. "I personally don't believe in a hierarchical system," says Jain. "Just because you are in a higher position at a company does not mean that others in a lower position should be viewed beneath you. I believe that heights were made to be looked at—not to be looked down from. When you reach a height it is not time to look down upon others. Let others look up at you and see how they can also reach up."

HOW DO YOU FIND YOUR INNER HUMILITY?

Our conception of humility as "insignificance" is inextricably linked to another attribute: self-confidence. Why? Because relinquishing feelings of self-importance in order to embrace "insignificance" requires prior confidence to do so. Look at Weber's story, for example. If Weber's commander had less confidence, he may have lacked the fortitude to share his mistake. Sharing this story, however, showed his inner humility, which had a beneficial effect on the mission. Similarly, you must have the self-confidence necessary to reveal your "insignificance."

Yet humility's prerequisite of self-confidence leads to an inherent contradiction: because feelings of self-importance are often signs of insecurity (which itself is a sign of poor self-confidence), many people with feelings of self-importance will lack the self-confidence required to dispose of their self-important feelings in the first place. It is, thus, especially difficult for self-important people to render themselves "insignificant." This is a serious problem, for self-important people are most in need of a dose of humility.

How can a self-important person find the genuine self-confidence to show humility? Everyone simply needs to develop his or her self-esteem—and, yes, this includes those of you who think you already have high self-esteem or think you are not self-important. You can always do better. Self-esteem can always be improved.

Now here is the real shocker: ironically, the best way to build your self-esteem is to make yourself vulnerable—the same act that often conveys humility as well (by humbly telling his story, Weber's commander certainly made himself vulnerable to criticism from the new crew, but their respect for him only increased). Yet, encouraging expressions of vulnerability (and, hence, humility) without first providing a way to build-up self-esteem and self-confidence seems an illogical prescription. The justification is simple, however: in order to begin expressing humility, you simply must jump in and begin.

You do not want to make yourself vulnerable in situations that will set you up for failure, in other words exposing your neck to a person with a dagger. You do want to make yourself *constructively vulnerable,* whereby you prepare yourself to benefit from your actions. This includes sharing stories of past mistakes and what you learned from them or simply being friendly and respectful to other people (yes, being friendly makes you vulnerable in that you may get shut down); but it does not include reckless maneuvers that serve little purpose other than embarrassment, such as openly detailing *every* blunder from your past. If you still worry about making yourself constructively vulnerable, try to have faith in people. Even if you leave your neck exposed, few people—even those holding daggers—are going to take advantage of you.

This somewhat complex concept of humility has yielded the following formula: constructive vulnerability both directly conveys humility and leads to higher self-esteem, which, in turn, creates higher self-confidence necessary to express even more humility.

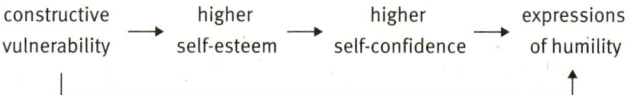

Overwhelmed? Take a moment for it all to sink in and consider the inspirational story of one of our interviewees, Jack Riopelle. In 1993, Riopelle became the president of Wisconsin Film & Bag, a custom packaging company. Whenever Riopelle went on the production floor, he noticed that employees never looked him in the eye. After probing the source of this behavior, he discovered that employees had become so accustomed to the previous owner's air of superiority that they now chose to keep their eyes down. Riopelle knew he wanted to change the culture of his workplace. He started with himself: he wanted people to know he cared about them. Realizing the power of small, yet calculated, expressions of humility, Riopelle stopped wearing a suit and tie and also made sure he never drove the most expensive car in the parking lot. Both were attempts to seem more accessible to his employees; both showed a definite "insignificance" towards his high position in the company. Riopelle also showed his personal side, making himself vulnerable to potential criticism from his fellow executives. "I laugh, I cry, I show empathy, I try to exhibit that I care for people," shares Riopelle. "And I think that real caring permeates an organization much more than most CEOs ever realize."

The result was a more cohesive company, in which employees with lower positions did not feel a great divide between management and themselves. To boot, none of the other executives criticized his actions. These actions transformed Riopelle's outlook on the role of CEOs and all leaders within a business. "CEOs often give the impression that they're the most important person in the company—that they're the ones who should be recognized and applauded," explains Riopelle. "But when you exhibit that kind of self-centeredness, you're not going to get loyalty from your employees." Indeed, there is little more inspiring or loyalty-begetting than a successful person, such as Riopelle, who is humble about his achievement.

Riopelle's humility helped bring about a family-like atmosphere to the company—a big ego, an inability to admit fault, or a lack of respect for others simply leads to insularity. Arrogant interpersonal actions often make others feel below you, creating distance between both parties; humble actions, on the other hand, put you and others on a plane of equal respect, where others feel comfortable around you—even if you are a superior. In a packaging industry traditionally focused only on maximizing efficient and cost-effective production, Jack Riopelle put an emphasis on conveying humility—and the benefit greatly outweighed the cost. In fact, there was no real cost.

More than setting the precedent within his industry, Riopelle sets himself apart from the entire business crowd. All too often, leaders today are stern figures that would sooner lose a limb than crack a smile or shed a tear. Yet effective leaders must let others in. They must admit that at times they are frightened to death. Why? Because employees need to see passion and compassion. They need to see exhilaration. They need to experience laughter. They need to see tears. They need to see the humanity of the leader. A mechanical, unduly macho leader only creates distance between him or her self and everyone else, and employees have difficulty developing a relationship with a leader who appears so removed.

"I've seen so many leaders who operate out of selfishness and greed," says Riopelle. "They rarely get buy-in from their employees, and they never get genuine respect from the people that they interact with because it's always, 'Me, me, me,' and not 'We, we, we.' The rash of disloyalty in the business world is in large part due to high-level executives who play the 'me' game instead of the 'we' game. Leadership doesn't mean that you have to be a braggart or carry around 200 pounds of testosterone."

Humility works best.

HOW DO YOU PRACTICE HUMILITY?

You have within you the power to express humility, daily and deeply. Allowing humility to permeate your everyday activities will produce a remarkable result: People will feel more confident approaching you and feel more excited to be in your company. Abide by the following eight guidelines for just a week, and you will notice the change. Mary Ellen Weber, Jack Riopelle, and Dipak Jain have already discovered the power of humility—you can, too!

Plan of Action

1. Express concern for others.
2. Take responsibility for your failures and learn from them.
3. Express gratitude for the good and bad—both are blessings!
4. Admit mistakes.
5. Apologize when you are wrong.
6. Give credit to others for their help in your success.
7. Show patience and forgiveness when treatment is unfair.
8. Be gracious when accepting feedback.

Contrary to the old model for success derived from money, control, and power, the new model for greatness centers on weaving humility into daily interaction. Charles Lewis, founder of the Center for Public Integrity, understands this model.

"There must be a willingness to recognize that even if you have an exciting, spectacular moment, when all the pistons are firing perfectly, those times are exceedingly rare, even in a successful organization," says Lewis. "You have to be continually self-critical and be willing to have a substantial degree of humility. If there is a prima donna, he can upset the energy of those around him."

Times when the "pistons are firing perfectly" are indeed rare. Humility is essential the rest of the time. Notice Lewis's focus on energy as well. People who embrace humility nurture the energy of those around them. They make an effort to listen to others and accept their individuality. They express concern for others, express gratitude, admit mistakes, apologize when wrong, give credit to others, show patience and forgiveness, and graciously accept feedback. They take responsibility for their own failures and learn from them. Wow! Now *that* is different—and more caring—energy. It is the energy of humility.

Perhaps Dipak Jain, in his characteristically venerable tone, captures the true essence of humility. "There is an analogy I like involving fruit," shares Jain. "The riper the fruit gets on a tree, it starts bending down towards the earth. As you go up in work and in life, you need to become more humble and more down to earth. You need to point more toward the earth than toward the sky." Indeed, the earth is what grounds us, provides stability, and because of gravity, keeps us upright. The same holds true for humility.

4

Compassion

"Compassion is the ultimate and most meaningful embodiment of emotional maturity. It is through compassion that a person achieves the highest peak and deepest reach in his or her search for self-fulfillment."
ARTHUR JERSILD

"Compassion is the keen awareness of the interdependence of all things."
THOMAS MERTON

"Your vision will become clear only when you look into your heart. Who looks outside, dreams. Who looks within, awakens."
CARL JUNG

Years ago, Randy Larrimore was working for a consulting company when it became clear that his mother was soon going to die. His boss said, "Be with your mother" and sent him home. The day after she passed away, Larrimore called to say he would be back at work immediately. His boss said, "No, take another week and be with your dad."

"I have never forgotten what he did for me and I thought it was just an amazing demonstration of caring for others," Larrimore says.

A few days after September 11th, Larrimore gathered his whole company by the flagpole in front of the building. He led the group in the Pledge of Allegiance and sang "God Bless America." They talked about the tragedy and reflected on the impact and how they should react.

Days later, an employee who had volunteered to leave the company asked to take back her resignation letter. She had been moved by the reaction to the tragedy and couldn't picture any other company caring as much about its employees.

Showing you care forms a lasting impression. "My motivation has a lot to do with truly caring," Larrimore explains. "I send birthday cards to probably 50 people a month. I write notes to people. I send e-mails to people when I think they have done a good job, and sometimes when they don't do a good job. I try to go out of my way to do something personal for somebody."

To Randy Larrimore, compassion is rooted in relationships. His constant efforts to be supportive and encouraging to his workers are an effective form of compassion. These small acts—cards, notes and e-mails—not only convey emotion, encouragement, support, and interest, but they help to steady employees during the tough times. Workers have an enhanced emotional connection to their organization.

WHAT IS COMPASSION?

Compassion is having a concern for the well-being of others. The word itself is from the Latin *cum patior,* to suffer with. It means understanding another person to such a degree that you can empathize entirely with his or her feelings and thoughts. A leader who is compassionate is kind, gracious, clement, generous, and nonjudgmental—not the common characteristics that you would find in most corporate leaders today. That is the whole point. We have all come to believe that the best role model is a person who is strong-willed, determined, emotionless, and firm. Yet, employees and customers feel far more comfortable with leaders who convey softness rather than hardness. A leader needs to believe that these "softer" qualities are not signs of weakness.

Compassion means to be in the heart of another person. The closer we are to others, the more we can feel or relate to their situation—

be in their hearts—and experience their emotions, whether happiness, confusion, sorrow, pain, or misery. Genuine compassion results in feeling concerned and responsible for another. It is not enough just to feel it; one must do something with it.

Leaders need to be authentic and genuine. This is why humility is the precursor to compassion. It opens a person up in a way that enables compassion to flow in and become real.

WHAT DOES COMPASSION LOOK LIKE?

Compassion can be observed on the faces of employees. They are engaged, they smile and laugh frequently, and they feel safe to speak honestly. This nurturing and kindhearted workplace adds texture to professional relationships because employees and managers deeply bond.

Moreover, compassionate relationships pull others in by listening and asking questions. There is a "culture of caring" within the organization that encourages people to flourish. Within this culture, success is defined by helping others. An employee asks, "Did I make them feel better about themselves? Did I make them feel like they were capable of achieving more than they ever thought they could?"

Manifesting Compassion

Compassion can be as simple as saying a kind word to a fellow employee. If there has been an organizational change, then it means sitting down to talk with the individuals involved and personally explaining the details; it means understanding how they feel and amplifying how they can add value.

Compassion can also be expressed on a greater scale, as Chris Zorich did, when he set up a foundation to serve the hungry and homeless. Zorich confides, "I believe that I've been put on this earth to help people that were in my circumstances before. The only difference between the person living in my neighborhood on the wrong side of the tracks, and the person who is CEO for a Fortune 500 company, is opportunity. When I left home, everyone kept beating it in my head that I came from the wrong neighborhood, but when I started living in better circumstances, I realized that the people I met were no better than the folks I grew up with. I want them to know they can achieve success too. When I walked away from football, I walked away from a million dollars a year. I just had this burning desire to affect change on a larger scale."

According to the Dalai Lama in his book *An Open Heart: Practicing Compassion in Everyday Life,* true compassion "has the intensity and spontaneity of a loving mother caring for her suffering baby. Throughout the day, such a mother's concern for her child affects all her thoughts and actions. This is the attitude we are working to cultivate with each and every being. When we experience this, we have generated great compassion." Zorich left his fans and football to care for a group that he came to know as a boy growing up without food and housing. His compassion is nurturing and pervasive, like that of a loving mother.

Individual Acts of Compassion

The act of compassion (remember—it's not just a thought) can be expressed individually in small ways. Randy Larrimore explains, "I feel my life's purpose is to leave the world a little better for having passed through it. When I went to college, my goal was to make the world better through chemistry. I decided after three years and qualifying for a chemistry major that it wasn't what I wanted to do. What I have found since then is there are other ways to make a difference. You don't have to invent a new polio vaccine. There are other things you can do to make the world better." He has discovered the phenomenal power of small expressions of compassion.

Larrimore likes to share a parable called *The Star Thrower* by author and anthropologist Loren Eisley. According to the tale, a man is walking along a beach and comes across a boy picking something up off the sand and gently throwing it into the ocean. Curious, the man asked, "What are you doing?"

"I am throwing starfish into the ocean," the boy answered. "The sun is up and the tide is going out and if I don't throw them in, they will die."

The man said, "Well, don't you realize there are miles and miles of beach and hundreds of starfish? You can't possibly make a difference."

The little boy bent down and he picked up another starfish and threw it into the surf. He smiled at the man and said, "But I made a difference to that one."

Larrimore tells his managers that their professional mission is not different from their life mission. If they can make a difference in the lives of their subordinates—no matter how small—they really will have accomplished something. This is because there is a cumulative impact of individual acts of compassion on employees, the organization, and their overall performance.

Just as small efforts are of great consequence, so too is the value of words. Astronaut Mary Ellen Weber stresses: "I have found that very often peoples' words of recognition are so important. I know personally when others have passed on words of thanks or recognized a job well done it has meant a lot. And very often it is so easy to do, but we assume they know they are doing a good job, they don't need to hear it. It is amazing how just a few words or a small gesture can help someone and change their day." Weber has hit on one of the top three ways to give compassion through recognition as we shall explain later in this chapter.

WHY ENGAGE IN COMPASSION?

Compassion brings compelling benefits to an organization and individuals. Recent research supports the value of compassion at work. A recent 2003 study, entitled "What Good Is Compassion at Work?," conducted by researchers at the University of Michigan Business School and the University of British Columbia Business School, advanced the notion that no matter how microscopic, acts of compassion are of great consequence in the workplace. The study also found that organizations that nurture compassion among employees often experience significant long-term benefits to commitment and productivity. Jane Dutton, a professor of business administration at the University of Michigan Business School, and Peter Frost, a professor of organizational behavior at the University of British Columbia's Faculty of Commerce and Business Administration, stress that small acts of compassion—as simple as patting someone on the shoulder, preparing a home-cooked meal for a sick co-worker, or easing someone's pain who is going through a crisis—make a huge difference. Whether you are on the giving end or the receiving end, such acts of compassion form impressions of your organization and these impressions last. Obviously, compassion can't happen unless it is accepted within the culture. It's up to leaders and co-workers to encourage compassionate understanding and acts of behavior. When others see that the organization supports compassion, it is a powerful motivator.

If organizations need economic reasons to encourage compassionate behavior, there are certainly some compelling ones! A growing body of evidence shows that an emphasis on managing and motivating people positively affects the harder traditional bottom line and gives a boost to hard measures including ROI, stock price, and operating earnings. Several books in recent years support this premise. *Why the Bottom Line Isn't!* and "Business and the Spirit: Management Practices That Sustain Values" in the *Handbook of Workplace Spirituality and Organizational Performance* are good examples that also place high value on the people within organizations.

The Road to Compassion Is through Other-Discovery, Not Self-Discovery

One of our favorite books on compassion is *Field Notes on the Compassionate Life: A Search for the Soul of Kindness*. The author, Marc Ian Barasch, says that the road to a compassionate life occurs through other-discovery rather than self-discovery. He quotes Father Thomas Keating, a Benedictine monk, who said, "The American Way is to first feel good about you, and then feel good about others. But spiritual traditions say it's really the other way around—that you develop a sense of goodness by giving of yourself."

Don't wait until your "self" is mature, developed, and happy to show compassion and give to others. Do it now, because the focus on giving to others emotes or leads to feeling good yourself.

It is no surprise that acts of kindness are a poignant and powerful web that unites one another in the workplace. Employees reward organizations that treat them well, too. When the Malden Mills manufacturing plant in Massachusetts burned to the ground in December 1995, the owner, Aaron Feuerstein, made the decision to rebuild his factory instead of putting the $300 million insurance payout in his pocket. He was determined to keep all 3,000 employees on his payroll for three months while he rebuilt. Productivity nearly doubled when the plant reopened. Feuerstein's unusual generosity and humane treatment certainly made an impact on his employees and in the long term rewarded his bottom line. It was all accomplished through kindness.

If Feuerstein can do it, so can others. Just as we encourage our children to express compassion within our families, we ought to teach the same lesson in the workplace. Leave a legacy of giving; make kindness a major part of your work life; take your gifts, personal and professional, and enrich your workplace; seek the extraordinary with your ordinary gifts; do as much as you can for others. This is how the workplace—and the world—improves.

HOW TO PRACTICE COMPASSION

The three steps in practicing compassion are: compassionate listening, compassionate talking, and recognition.

Compassionate Listening

One of the most powerful and effective ways to express compassion is by deep listening. Sadly, deep listening is a lost art, especially with the increased use of e-mail, cell phones, and voicemail. To get a feel for the skill required for deep listening, think of the speaker and listener as playing a game of Frisbee. A Frisbee can be awkward to throw accurately because of its rim and radius. Frisbees can also be thrown so that they intentionally curve—just like many conversations. Listening deeply is like catching the Frisbee. You have to pay attention, focus on the thrower, anticipate where it is going to be thrown, be ready to leap to catch it wherever it goes, and finally make the catch. It requires the complementary skills and efforts of both players, appropriately attuned to each other.

Look at the roles of speaker and listener. The speaker must observe the listener attentively, looking for "indicators" as to whether he or she is listening. The listener must also observe the speaker and express feelings of warmth and enthusiasm. Compassionate listeners will communicate that they are engaged in a number of ways. Physical contact—a smile even—conveys good listening. Acknowledgment is a key action that often signals compassion. Their eyes are alert and they nod their head. They ask questions, verbally acknowledge that they have understood an idea, and add information. Good listeners apply the general information they hear to more specific situations.

Not everyone knows when they are speaking to an active listener. Though some of us stop talking when we discover that someone is not listening, most adults continue talking even though there are no signs that someone else is listening! We have forgotten how to observe the listener. Good speakers know when their audience is not there to catch their words.

Check your own listening skills. Ask yourself:

- Am I attentive?
- Do I accept the speaker and the situation?
- Do I clarify and try to understand?
- Are my views changing or being supported?

If you follow these guidelines, you will listen deeply and compassionately. You might also do better at catching a Frisbee. Learn to listen actively and compassionately so that you can catch each thought when someone talks to you.

Compassionate Talking

Effective compassion is rooted in words. In his classic book, *Teacher and Child,* child psychotherapist Dr. Haim Ginott offers guidance to teachers and parents on how to talk to children. Their language, he stresses, tells children how they feel about them, and to a large extent, affects their self-worth and self-esteem. Their statements determine their destiny. We can apply Ginott's thinking on how to talk to adults. Leaders must take a close look at their language and be aware of the impact of words. Compassionate talk fosters interpersonal relationships. There is an unselfish sense of connection and commitment. Its value is huge!

The famous educational philosopher John Dewey said that learning involves the representation of one's experiences. If we encourage a person to talk in a group—family, school, or workplace—then that person learns. The person represents his or her experiences and begins to understand them. When a person hears other people talking; his or her understanding is also enlarged.

Think back to the definition of compassion—to be in the heart of another person—and consider the value of talk in this sense. Consider the value of open communication. Don't restrict the boundaries of conversation. Let workers know it's good to grow individually in different areas and directions. Always encourage active listening and you'll learn from each other. Be open, direct, and deep. Describe problems, give information, encourage dialogue, and don't forget to model how to do it. Fully express your own feelings, needs, and expectations. Talk about everything and nothing—from racial discrimination and its causes to your favorite foods and how you prepare them. Share your past experiences, good and bad, and what you learned. It will inspire your employees to share theirs, now and as they spend more time together. Walk down unknown conversational paths. Feel safe doing the unsafe. Let this kind of deep talk nourish you. It will create rich and rare relationships.

Learning to talk deeply creates a rare and wonderful energy between others. Imagine what work would be like if there were no talking. In authoritarian work environments, employees are afraid to say anything, so there is silence. Workers quickly learn that they must be seen and not heard. Meaningful communication is rare. Yelling, the worst form of verbalization, is too common.

Close and healthy work environments are built through frequent, open, two-way communication—and lots of it. Try to talk on a regular basis, especially at meetings when everyone is sitting together. Establish a ritual where workers go around the table and talk about the most meaningful—or discouraging—part of their work. This may be an event, a personal project, or a thought—anything that has special importance. Try to break free from old and repeated topics. It's good to change your conversational patterns. Open up new thoughts, dream out loud, share private tears, and explore perspectives on everything—from failures to fears. Compassionate talking can be effortless, if you let it be.

Furthermore, don't forget to laugh! A 1996 news report said that children laugh approximately 400 times a day while adults only laugh about 15 times. Social scientists who study humor want to better understand why 385 laughs vanish. These same laugh researchers also note the medical benefits of laughter. Laughing relieves stress, controls pain, lowers blood pressure, provides an aerobic workout for the diaphragm, improves the body's ability to utilize oxygen, and maximizes the flow of disease-fighting proteins and cells in the blood. For health reasons alone, it sounds like adults need more laughs. Laughter strengthens the insides, physically and emotionally.

Recognition

Teachers and parents give recognition and positive feedback all the time—isn't it peculiar that we have omitted it from our work settings? Over a lifetime, we spend as much time—or more—at work as we do at home and in school. When we tell our children, "You've done a great job," their faces light up, and when they send back a smile, they reward us for our recognition. Work settings must do the same for employees. Providing recognition is as rewarding to the giver as it is to the receiver. After a while, giving recognition becomes as self-satisfying as receiving it.

A verbal thank you, of course, is the easiest and quickest recognition to give. When was the last time you wrote a brief note thanking the people who helped you with an assignment? Can you describe what they did particularly well? Maybe they will even write one to you, expressing gratitude for the opportunity to work with you.

Recognition is different from providing feedback to an individual. Recognition personally conveys a sense of appreciation and continued encouragement. It's fine for the focus of recognition to be the completed task, but for recognition to provide maximum benefit, it's important to have the individual feel greater self-worth—not just satisfaction about the action being recognized.

Recognition can be offered in a variety of ways and under different circumstances. It can be given for an employee's insight for identifying a problem, acknowledging the difficulties the employee encountered while solving the problem, and understanding the benefits of the employee's solution. Providing positive reinforcement to employees along the way is far more motivating than waiting until the task has been accomplished.

An effective leader always seeks ways to provide recognition, yet so often we woefully under-recognize others. We hear managers lament, "But, you don't want to make people feel overconfident or think they're too good and then they'll be asking you for more money." How naïve! When it's genuine and legitimate, recognition doesn't cause ego-inflation; rather, it strengthens an individual's inner core. It enables them to feel better about themselves and in turn to perform more effectively and efficiently. When people are filled with self-doubt and question themselves, they underperform. Their concentration becomes fragmented because they spend time and energy wondering if their actions will be recognized.

Team or group leaders need to give far more thought to effective ways to provide their team members with recognition. However, group members also have a responsibility to provide their leaders with positive recognition and reinforcement. Most people expect the flow of recognition to stem from the top down. How often have you complimented your boss for a job well done? Probably not often. Yet, providing recognition to those at the top can be enabling and motivating for them. Providing frequent recognition is beneficial because it leaves groups stronger, more confident, and better motivated to perform productively, focusing on the tasks at hand rather than worrisome self-doubt.

••

Promoting a Life of Compassion

Virginia Duncan Gilmore
Founder of the Sophia Foundation

"I believe in the values of authenticity and vulnerability, and I call that being real," says Virginia Duncan Gilmore.

Everything was crashing down on Gilmore at once, and she didn't know what to do. She had decided to leave the fourth-generation family company she helped to lead. She was in the midst of a divorce, and to make things even more challenging, her daughter was headed off to college.

Her career was over. Her home was empty. She was alone, confused, and scared.

Like Thoreau before her, Gilmore escaped to the woods to find herself. She found her own "Walden Pond" in northeast Wisconsin and stayed for two months. Each day she would wake up, go for a walk, and write in her journal. She would look into the majestic waters of Lake Michigan, watch the autumn leaves turn colors and fall to the ground, and let nature comfort her and provide clarity.

"When I had three life changes come at once, I was just immobilized. I simply had to get off the merry-go-round. My inner needs were so strong at that point I just had to stop and deal with them."

So for two months, Gilmore stopped. Then she started anew. She was able to get in touch with a part of her that she had neglected, a part that she had buried through work.

In 1998, Gilmore co-founded the Center for Spirituality and Leadership at Marian College in Fond du Lac, Wisconsin. The Center "promotes leadership that nurtures the gifts and spirit of each person and cultivates caring community environments in which persons become more whole, healthy, creative, and dedicated to service."

Not long after, Gilmore founded the Sophia Foundation, an organization that works in communities to create systemic change to promote the dignity of all human beings with a special focus on women and children. In its first four years, the foundation had given grants of more than $325,000 to groups that represent the values of compassion, spirituality, wholeness, community, transformation, and stewardship.

Her value set begins with compassion. Ginny Gilmore sees a future where men and women are compassionate in their dealings with employees, friends, family, and even strangers. Compassion is the key to unlocking a sense of community. It is the cornerstone for success.

••

Respecting the Sacred Person

There is a difference between giving someone attention and giving them respect. Often leaders will pay lip-service to individuals, pretending they care, but viewing them simply as a means to an end. Gilmore understands that to truly respect someone is to recognize their uniqueness as an individual.

"I hope people see my values in the way that I relate to others," Gilmore shares. "I hope they feel safe with me so they can tell me what they really care about, and I hope they feel that if there is something wrong in our relationship they can tell me that. I just hope they know that I really respect them as a sacred person. I want others to see me giving my time, my self, and my financial resources to what I care about most."

It is easy to be there physically in a relationship, but it is much more difficult to make yourself available to people. It requires that you give them your time, attention, and feelings. However, it is only when you are willing to make that effort for others that you can truly effect change together.

"Human dignity and justice are certainly important values to me," Gilmore says. "I say being available in a relationship, that's the same as being present. You must recognize other people as equal, sacred, and purposeful, and then it is important for you to work with others to take action that changes the system."

Searching for Wonder

One of the greatest challenges a leader faces is moving beyond what he or she already knows. We cling to what we have read, what we have been taught, and who we have met. We form an idea of how we perceive things must be. However, this restrictive frame of reference is a crutch, preventing us from seeing anything but what is already there.

"Letting go of whatever keeps you from something new, whether it's fear or whether it's a belief, creates the space for you to know something different," Gilmore states.

When you let go, when you accept that things can be different, you can unleash innovative ideas. This is not the result of serendipity or accident. To develop a new way of thinking takes a conscious effort to expose you to new things, to ask questions and search for answers.

Gilmore adds, "I think wonder is really important. And I think that in order to really keep that top-of-mind, it is really important for me to connect with beauty, and that can be art and music and nature and children and love, and all those kinds of things. You must continually ask 'What do you wonder about?' It is so powerful to invite yourself to wonder and encourage others to wonder."

A simple question can yield tremendous power. To invite others to wonder is to invite them to be more than what they already are and empower them to see a better future that you can work together to achieve. To help people see into themselves and their future is an act of compassion.

Generating Energy through Learning

As people age, there is a tendency to stop learning. However Gilmore knows that this attitude leads to apathy; education is the impetus for action. She says, "Continual learning is really an energy generator for me and I think it's also a practice for me, because if you really practice dialogue, you hold your judgments aside and you listen to somebody else. I think the learning helps open me up to thinking differently."

The moment we stop learning is the moment that we stop listening. It is the moment in which we boast that we know enough, and what we know is right. No individual can or should ever reach that point. Instead, we should cherish our opportunities to learn and grow.

"I value deep listening," Gilmore says, "which has been probably the most important capacity that I have been developing through dialogue and also my own spiritual practice, listening to my inner self, listening at a deep level to others and really hearing myself and others."

Sometimes we are so used to shutting people out that we need to train ourselves to listen—and there is so much out there to listen to: friends, family, colleagues, teachers, and certainly our own hearts and minds. The more you listen, the clearer things become.

Accepting Pain to Bring Joy

Our lives are filled with joy and pain. The birth of children is met by the death of parents. However, the sorrow we feel at a loss provides us the perspective to cherish our gifts and blessings.

"Even though human life has a lot of pain in it, what I believe is that pain and joy are different sides of the same coin, and if I don't know pain, I won't know joy," Gilmore shares. "Joy is the invitation."

Painful experiences also allow us to develop empathy, the ability to understand the situations of others. Powerful leaders do not just recognize the struggles of those around them, but they also connect with them in meaningful ways.

"The experiences that I have had in life that were challenging and difficult were both very painful and healing," Gilmore confides. "Those experiences give me the opportunity to relate to you when you are having those experiences, most effectively, most intimately."

Sharing Compassion

Great leaders recognize that compassion begins from within. Only when individuals can forgive themselves and love themselves, can they give that forgiveness and love to others. It is a difficult task because we will all stumble through our life's journey.

Leaders fail just like everyone else; however, what strengthens them is the ability to learn from that failure to help them and their teams succeed in the future. We have all been knocked down before; a great leader is always there to help you get back up.

Gilmore says, "I think it's really important for somebody to step up and say, 'You know I really fell once.' I really fell down and was in the process of getting up when I recognized that I had some gifts along the way. It was through that process that I discovered who I was and what I cared about and how to live the rest of my life."

Gilmore believes that you learn more on the way up than you do at the top. It is only when you have nothing that you can learn what is truly meaningful to you.

Calling Forth the Gifts of Others

Leaders see things in people. They see their strengths and weaknesses. They see their passions and fears. They see what makes them special and work to draw that out.

We all have something special within us that may be buried or hidden, but it is powerful nonetheless. It is only through developing a meaningful relationship with an individual that you can draw that gift out. In so doing, compassion is once again made evident.

"You discern other people's values by looking at the way they live their lives," Gilmore believes. "I listen to how they relate, I watch how they interact with others. There's an energy there that I can feel."

That energy is compassion.

5

Transparency

"I still think you can't even get close to solve the problems, if you don't get the truth. I've been studying Katrina. That's a great case where the government tried to hide the truth, and it didn't work."

CHARLES LEWIS, founder of the Center for Public Integrity

Soon after he became president of his previous company Jack Riopelle learned that it was common practice within his industry to cheat customers. Marketed materials were often substituted for less expensive, inferior products—and customers were never told. It would have been easy for him to change this practice quietly, but doing things behind closed doors had never been Riopelle's style. He spoke to members of his corporate office and shared his findings with them, noting that this so-called "material swap" had been going on for quite some time. They responded very positively and agreed that the problem had to be fixed. An internal audit lasted about three months, after which Riopelle forced his salespeople, who were actively involved in the scheme, to offer refund checks to customers and to explain why they were getting them. Sales representatives were required to obtain signature verifications of receipt from customers to whom they gave the checks. As you can imagine, the 88 salespeople resisted this directive because it meant admitting they had been participants in dishonest activity.

Yet to Riopelle's delight, his company did not lose a single customer. In fact, Riopelle received calls and letters praising his integrity and the honesty of his organization. The decision to take this action was tough, unpopular, and could have alienated Riopelle from his employees. In his mind, however, there was no other option. "Lots of people talk about integrity, and it is easy to talk the talk, but not necessarily walk the walk," explains Riopelle. "Every day, leaders are faced with issues that challenge them to consistently act with integrity. If they cannot always act with 100-percent integrity, the ability of people to follow and trust those leaders gets compromised."

WHAT IS TRANSPARENCY?

Transparency is rooted in two Latin words: *trans,* meaning across or through, and *parere,* meaning to show. Transparency, then, can be translated to mean "to show through." Other definitions include "easily seen or detected," "obvious," "candid," and "open."

Transparency means sharing information—both good and bad. It is about laying everything on the table for everyone to see, evaluate, and—if warranted—criticize. The benefits are substantial, however. With a willingness to open up comes an environment of trust and candidness like that of Riopelle's post-audited firm, one in which everyone finds it easy to have honest relationships based on the clarity of knowing where people stand and how they feel. Hidden agendas simply cannot exist when openness, fairness, and a sense of integrity are part of an organization's culture.

WHAT DOES TRANSPARENCY LOOK LIKE?

There are three types of transparency essential to leadership: business, governmental, and individual. In business, transparency is openly portraying financial data so that employees and shareholders grasp the numbers. Transparent procedures include budgetary reviews, open meetings, audits, financial disclosure statements, and freedom of information legislation. Jack Riopelle made it a mission, for instance, to increase drastically the level of business transparency within his company.

In government, transparency is reflected in the public's ability to participate in the political process. The governed deserve to know what decisions are made, which actions are taken, and the underlying reasons why. While people understand that the CIA and Department of Defense may need to keep secrets, better communication regarding what is actually happening within government circles, along with an open rationale on budget decisions and allocations, is necessary to understand what happens behind all-too-often closed political doors.

For the individual, transparency is being completely open, straightforward, and direct on a personal level.

Another aspect of business transparency needs elaboration. Indeed, Jack Riopelle's story demonstrated the need for financial transparency, but what about fostering the transparency of corporate goals? What can be done to encourage greater openness and sharing of information, dialogue, and decisions? The answer is to identify and articulate the collective values of the people within the organization. When an organization exposes its values to its own employees, then the opaque organizational cover turns into see-through glass. As soon as a group's values have been clarified, the behaviors and communications will also be more open, expansive, and ultimately transparent.

Consider the following example. Something truly unprecedented just occurred at IBM. For the first time since the company's founding, all 319,000 IBMers around the globe were invited to make transparent their company's goals in an online "values jam" that lasted 72 hours. Tens of thousands contributed to a free-flowing dialog that examined all the "stuff" that was getting in the way of serving clients, implementing new ideas, and working as a global team. President and

CEO Samuel Palmisano led the jam. He felt as if his "troops" needed to affirm their reason for being in the firm—namely, what set IBM apart and which core values should drive its actions. Consensus produced three values:

- Dedication to every client's success
- Innovation that matters, for IBM and the world
- Trust and personal responsibility in all relationships

The benefits of making transparent these core values are seemingly limitless. Doing so united the IBM company workforce, helping to rid employees of a sense of isolation that can come from working for such a large corporation. It also made people feel as if their voices had been heard by allowing them to determine what is important to the company. Moreover, because the values were not dictated from the highest level, employees did not feel hammered by excessive controls. As one can see, defining a company's values not only serves as a compass for future decisions and behavior, but also builds community by pinpointing what everyone finds important.

WHAT ARE THE BENEFITS OF TRANSPARENCY?

As stories about political corruption monopolize headlines; it becomes clear that government sorely needs transparency. Meet Charles Lewis. He is America's watchdog for transparency in both the public and private sectors. *The Village Voice* appropriately labeled Lewis "the Paul Revere of our time," for he has dedicated his life to responsible journalism on issues of public concern. Committed to transparent and comprehensive reporting, he founded and was for 15 years the executive director of the Center for Public Integrity. He was also a professor of journalism at Princeton and a research fellow at Harvard University, and currently teaches at American University.

Crusading for the Truth

Charles Lewis
Founder of Investigative Reporting Workshop at American University

Charles Lewis learned his finest lesson in junior high school. A guidance counselor told him not to bother going to college because he was not a serious student. He was later told by the University of Delaware that he would likely flunk out in the first semester. He learned not to believe everything he heard. He graduated with honors and distinction, received a master's degree from Johns Hopkins University, and in l998, he won the prestigious John D. and Catherine T. MacArthur Foundation Fellowship. After he received the award, his mother sent the announcement to his junior high school guidance counselor.

Lewis is motivated by an ardent view that public and private officials need to be truthful through-and-through. His passion for truth has guided his investigative reporting over the past few decades, although it is also why Lewis is so worried about what is happening to the media. He believes that reporters often cannot out-power the political maneuvers of sly officials. "If given the truth, people can meet any crisis," he says, "but deception and manipulation are so thick these days, probably thicker than we've ever seen them, very possibly in history. The means for manipulation and the use of public moneys in terms of propaganda—public officials all saying the same thing on the same day, for instance—creates a din so loud that competent journalism is outmatched." Furthermore, he believes that it is increasingly difficult for good journalists to do good work. "More than two-thirds of journalists believe media owners have sold them out and will act and behave, at times, in unethical and compromising ways," he says. "The number of reporters at some newspapers is half of what they were 20 years ago. More outlets cover less substantive news, which means we are going to be more reliant on the government and corporate institutions to tell us what their 'truth' is, and that becomes the 'new truth.'"

Transparency requires people keeping themselves informed and up-to-speed on current and world events. An informed point of view is where transparency begins. Today, however, a deadly situation exists—we do not have an informed public. More people know about the Three Stooges than the three branches of government; 40 percent of Americans cannot identify the name of the vice president; 11 percent of Americans cannot even identify the United States on a map of the world. The problem is deep-seated, according to Lewis. "We have been anaesthetized by media public relations efforts and basic propaganda with self-serving objectives," he claims. "We are cynical. We do not even believe that there are such things as objective facts and truths. We believe that everything has an agenda. Most people think newspapers, as we know them today, the physical product, will cease to exist. It is not if, but when—how many years will it take? The challenge is that, on the one hand, the Internet's accumulation of new data and Web sites each day creates world-wide information that is transparent and accessible to everyone. But this digital-demand information actually means the public is less informed; sports and crossword puzzles can be pulled down on personal computers, rather than hard news. On the other hand, the media and government are manipulating and shaping the data in ways that make it difficult to know the 'real' truth. What should the public know?"

This is where Lewis's Center for Public Integrity comes in. The Center is the international expert at tracking undue political influence and old-fashioned corruption both inside and outside the United States. Since its founding in 1989, the nonpartisan Center has produced roughly 300 investigative reports and 14 books, including the national bestseller, *The Buying of the President 2004*. The Center first disclosed that Enron was George W. Bush's top career patron. In 2003, it posted online the major U.S. contracts relating to the Iraq and Afghanistan wars online; these revealed that Halliburton had received more money in contracts than any other company. Center reports have been honored 35 times with national journalism awards.

Lewis's crusade for the truth has often infuriated those who participated in the corruption he exposed. The Center was even sued by Russian oligarchs.

"So many corporations would like to squish us," says Lewis. "We were up against presidents and speakers of the house. And we had to be extremely careful. We had the added pressure of doing things right, and then withstanding legal and financial threats. We did have a sense of being up against the wall at times. It wasn't an imaginary sales pitch to the staff; *we were under siege*. At one point we had three libel suits brought within 18 months (all later dismissed). There was some question of whether or not we'd survive. Instead, during that time we turned out 150 reports, wrote three books, and won a slew of national awards."

A Focus on Transparency

While Charles Lewis is still interested in holding public and private entities accountable for their actions, he has a new focus: examining what, precisely, government officials are saying. Lewis has begun analyzing the effects of public officials' lies—not simply reporting on them. He wants to get to the real truth and create a transparent view of what happens behind political doors. One of his main findings is that public officials have an incredible ability to mold history for personal gain, regardless of the actual facts. He explains: "At the Center we watched what public officials did, not what they said on the assumption that the officials were frequently lying. I came to see that it unfortunately doesn't matter what the officials did because you'll find it out after the fact. It's useful for historical purposes to find out what they did, but no matter what you find, the fact of the matter is that the public has such a fleeting interest and knowledge of what's happening, most of what officials have done will be defined by them. *It'll become the truth.* They'll put names on it like 'No Child Left Behind' or the 'Patriot Act.' And journalists feel the need to repeat the name of the legislation because that's what they want us to call it. I've come to the view that I have to reluctantly turn to the issue of what people say because it soon becomes reality. It's become perceived truth even though it's not true. It's very irritating; it makes my blood boil."

Achieving Organizational Transparency

Given the quantity and quality of work the Center produces, most people have no idea how a single man led the Center for Public Integrity for so long. Besides working 100-hour workweeks, Lewis led the Center with a commitment to organizational transparency similar to that of Riopelle. Yet to the mix of truth and transparency, Lewis added a touch of personal care. "I have always tried to treat people in a sensitive and fair way," he says. "Whatever we're doing right now, there should be a sense of mission and a sense of doing something important, and we're in it together. You have to have that sense of community internally. You don't if one person has some kind of ridiculous advantage, and doesn't pull his or her weight. And if everyone believes you're in it together and it's a deeply embedded sense of what it should be, they're going to want to participate because they'll see it's fair."

Treating people fairly, understanding their individual needs, and building a community of people who share similar values fosters transparency within organizations. In the 15 years during which he ran the Center, Charles did not have a single employee action taken (lawsuit or even threatened lawsuit). Even with over 250 employees including paid interns, he made it a point to take each person out to breakfast or lunch to get to know them personally. They knew that he cared about them, and they could hear from him what was going on. He also made sure each of them was mentored along the way. He had a core middle staff that would interact with the incoming interns. "When they know you're trying and care, it's huge," he says. Every year when he welcomed the interns, he would explain the Center and its mission. Then, he would say that he had worked in television, a profession in which they stab you in the front and not the back; he hated backbiting and games that people play, and if that was something that people enjoyed, leave today; if anyone was having a problem, he or she should come directly to the boss. "We know you're smart, but you also have to be nice, or you're not working here," he would tell interns. "You can't check resumes for nice; it's not on there. We didn't always choose the interns; the schools would; and the good news is that if you didn't have someone who fit in that way, they would only be there for ten weeks. You're assembling a group of like-minded folks when it comes to values, and if people have wildly divergent values, it'll be a nightmare. You're not going to get anything done. There won't be a sense of mission; there'll be continual negativity and negative energy."

HOW DO YOU PRACTICE TRANSPARENCY?

Historically, business leaders have tried to hide or distance themselves from failure. It is often easier to tell people what they want to hear or what you think you are supposed to say. Leaders feel the need to project a completely positive outlook regardless of reality. It is this logic that leads people down a slippery slope toward inflated earnings statements and cover-ups. Look at the fall of Enron, Tyco, and WorldCom, three companies that concealed their failures only to have them explode into company-breaking scandals; they chose not to be transparent about their failures.

Promoting a Transparent Life

Joel Hall
Founder of the
Joel Hall Dance Center

Yet there is an alternative way to deal with failure. Consider the story of Joel Hall, who for more than 30 years has served as artistic director of the Joel Hall Dance Center, Chicago's longest-thriving multicultural dance company and training center. Walk into the company's studio on Chicago's north side any day of the week and you will find toddlers tapping their feet to the music, and seniors peeling back the years as they move gracefully around the rooms. You will also find Hall teaching, motivating, and inspiring his diverse groups of students who travel from around the region to learn from the man whose lessons extend beyond the dance floor. Furthermore, if you ask him the correct body position for a pirouette or about any of his past hardships, Hall is sure to give you an honest, transparent answer. Yet Hall's current success did not come without substantial potholes in the road.

More than ten years ago, his building housing the Joel Hall Dancers burned to the ground. All of the dance group's information was lost as the fire reduced the once vibrant structure to a charred shell. There was no insurance. There was no plan for recovery. Nevertheless, two days later, Hall was directing his dancers in an abandoned studio in downtown Chicago. He had received a phone call from the parent of a former student who had danced with Hall 20 years before, and this person had offered to let him use the space. Several years later, Hall was met with tragedy again. He suffered a devastating loss when his partner in life and in business, passed away. His partner had handled the financial side of the company, allowing Hall to be the creative force. The death was very difficult for Hall and he questioned his desire to go forward with his work. "And it was a struggle for me, a personal struggle, with whether or not I wanted to continue with this loss of my other half," he said.

••

Don't miss our point here. Hall's misfortunes aren't what we are emphasizing. The key idea is that he readily lays his feelings, suffering, misfortune, and personal learning on the table. To him, transparency involves sharing information, both good and bad. It means putting one's self out there for everyone to see, assess, and possibly, pass judgment on. Hall's life is transparent. He knows difficulties can't be resolved if you hide the truth. Always candid and straightforward, never secretive, he is in alignment with what he says and how he acts.

There are moments in life and business that challenge our will. There are periods of adversity that seem insurmountable. One has a choice—dwell on the difficulty or move on to find a solution. An effective leader always recognizes the difference between a negative situation and a negative outlook. Just as he had picked everything up and started over when his studio burned down, Hall did not succumb to any desire to quit after his partner died. He chose to deal with this tragedy—to talk openly and transparently about it—rather than cover it up, pretend like it hadn't happened or simply abandon his current way of life. For Hall, to quit after his partner had died would be the ultimate failure: "The thing that we shared together was life and how we should live—and not how we should die," he reveals. "So when he died, I made sure that I lived. I learned the value of life, so that as an organization we were able to pick ourselves up in a matter of days, and continue what it is that we were supposed to be about, which was the business of dance, the business of the arts."

Nowadays ask Joel Hall about either of these hardships and he will be completely open about them, for his transparency reaches a deeply personal level. What made Hall choose openness, transparency, and acceptance of loss over so-called "pulling an Enron?" In other words, what allows Joel Hall to be so open? Hall possesses three qualities that give him this power: self-respect, adaptability, and a loving mind-set. The following sections discuss each of these qualities.

Quality One: Self-Respect

Hall's life is about truth and openness. He knows you can't get close and solve problems if you conceal the truth. Always transparent and honest, Hall is open to feelings, suffering, and misfortune. A sense of personal integrity permeates his interactions. There is not a different set of rules for different people. He is transparent with everyone.

Joel Hall's role with the JHDC encompasses much more than lending his name. His personality helps define the company. As an African-American who grew up in an underserved community, Hall has battled stereotypes and low expectations all his life. The result is an individual who is very aware of his abilities and what he has to offer.

Transparency starts with self-respect. Without a minimum level of self-confidence it becomes hard to act and speak with integrity. Says Hall: "I think respect for myself is one of my most important core values. Being an African-American man and coming from the area of the world that I came from, I think that learning self-respect and what that means was one of the first things I had to do. It certainly is not innate. What we really have to learn is that above all, when everything else fails, there is only you. It boils down to how you respect yourself, and I have a great, great respect for myself. I have learned how to do that over the years."

Hall concedes that the assertiveness, self-confidence, and brutal honesty that effective leaders display can be potentially intimidating to others. He recognizes that there can be a desire for a leader to change his or her way in reaction to this response. However, he feels that it is important to "stay in character" to retain credibility and self-respect. This focus on self-respect drives Hall in his life and work. He makes sure that, despite the results, his effort and intention is always something he can take pride in. Self-respect is closely linked to transparency. A person needs to feel good inside before he or she is willing and able to open up to others. When self-respect is in place, transparency can flourish.

Quality Two: Adaptability

If a person is rigid, closed, and inflexible, it will be impossible to be transparent. With an adaptive mind-set, transparency can emerge. As Hall explains, "One of our greatest attributes as humans is that of adaptation, and adaptation to me is the savior of the world. I use the word 'adapt' purely in understanding other ideas, being able to open yourself up, and not to say that you already know. The ability to say 'let's look at that.' And then after looking at something say whether or not we can accept or not accept it." Indeed, few things in the natural world are static. Life itself is a series of ever-changing people, places, and roles. Individuals who embrace change are better equipped to deal with it as it occurs.

Yet this is easier said than done. As Hall explained, the natural tendency is for individuals to adopt opinions and positions they are comfortable with, rather than expand their horizons into new areas. "People are so limited in terms of their perspective of things, that they put these visors on," he says. "They are not able to see over the flap. They are only looking one way and they can't look another, and that's a real problem in an organization."

Hall credits the diversity of his experiences with his ability and willingness to adapt to changing circumstances. He realized very early in his life that people were not necessarily going to change for him. Instead of limiting his options to situations that were safe and comfortable, Hall decided that he would open himself to learn and adapt. "Depending upon where I was at a particular situation in time, I had to cope with certain problems, and my morals developed from each of those areas that I had to evaluate and that I had to deal with," he shares. "That varies from being a footpad maker for a Dr. Scholl's factory to making heat massagers, to managing a community discount store on 47th and Halsted Streets, to managing a Zoom-Zoom Restaurant in New York City. So, different areas of my life have taken me different places, and in each area I have worked with many, many, many different kinds of people with various values and various attitudes. And being a chameleon one has to adapt to any situation that they are in and be very flexible."

Quality Three: A Loving Mind-set

If Hall's long-term partner had taught him anything, it was the importance of love. Love, too, is crucial for enabling transparency—for if someone is selfish, it is easy to think just as the Enron executives did and to hide personal failure behind a veil of lies. "The most valuable life lesson I learned was from my ex-partner, Joseph," said Hall, "and that was the idea of unconditional love. It radically changed me because I learned that I could offer it to others. My life had been all about survival before and so was his. But I really learned from him to have a loving approach to life, to not be selfish and be pretty direct, and it has helped me tremendously. So it has changed me in that I can now have a partner and say that I love you unconditionally and whatever we go through we will deal with. And I can say that to my organization as well, and it will endure." Indeed, Hall's love for his partner, his dancing, and for life allowed him to overcome adversity the right way—transparently.

6

Inclusiveness

> "To escape isolation, a person must be able to
> become a member of a group, and this is not
> just a problem of finding a group.
> The capacity for relating one's self easily to
> other men and women is not inborn,
> but a result of experience and training,
> and that experience and training is itself social."
>
> **GEORGE HOMANS** in *The Human Group*

Dipak Jain serves on the board of directors of John Deere and Company, yet he does not know how to drive a car let alone a tractor. He has consulted for IBM, Motorola, and U.S. Cellular, yet prefers old-fashioned technology. He is charged with molding the next generation of business leaders, a traditionally bloodthirsty lot, yet he is a vegetarian who preaches nonviolence.

Introspective and humble, Dipak Jain seems an unlikely choice to guide those aspiring to reach the upper echelons of the corporate world. Yet, since taking over as dean of Northwestern University's Kellogg School of Management in July 2001, Jain has utilized his global perspective and commitment to innovation to build the program's reputation as the world's premier business school. Kellogg was voted the "Best Business School" a record five consecutive times in *Business Week*'s survey of U.S. business schools. Jain views inclusiveness as a core value—one that can be seen when he often greets others with a hug. He demonstrates that even in the cutthroat world of business, valuing the diverse perspectives and contributions of all people is what effective and values-based leadership is all about.

WHAT IS INCLUSIVENESS?

Inclusiveness means being recognized and accepted as part of a whole. It means to include and take into account. Individuals who convey inclusiveness are open and respectful of differences, fully embrace who they are as human beings, and view others as a valuable part of the "team." Leaders who are effective at instilling inclusiveness strive to acknowledge and act upon the needs of others and communicate the value of their perspectives, thoughts, and opinions.

Inclusiveness should be relatively simple to activate within an organization, but for several reasons it is not. We seem to have certain biases and prejudices about others. As adults, we tend to exclude certain individuals more readily and frequently. When we do not understand others, we tend to feel inferior or superior to them.

The crucial requisite for inclusiveness is to deny all forms of discrimination—period. There are no excuses or rationalizations for being unfair to another person. At times, people position themselves above the fray, making others appear to have flaws or deficiencies in order to make themselves look good. Often, the motive to exclude is subconscious. We need to become more aware of subtle exclusion. Inclusiveness means becoming conscious of our differences, accepting them, celebrating them, and then trusting others.

Effective leaders possess the ability to get the most out of the individuals they work with in a positive and proactive way. They understand that cultivating the talents of those around them is one of the most powerful ways to move an organization forward. They recognize that the more you can make people feel included and valued, the more they will contribute.

Lifting People Up

Not only do effective leaders grasp the value of inclusiveness, they take it to the ultimate—they lift people up.

Dipak Jain
Dean of INSEAD

"I strongly believe that when you work with people you need to know how to lift them up," says Jain. "You need to create an environment where people feel that you really inspire and lift them to a higher level. In turn, they should feel good working with you because they know they will be valued. They will also have an opportunity to move up—professionally, personally, and emotionally. The whole concept of an environment that lifts people up is very important. It lets those around you see that working together helps everyone rise together, and that is where you develop a sense of inclusiveness with your people."

Jain believes that the key is to view others in a business as working *with* you and not *for* you. When leaders consider themselves separate from other employees, they create inherent conflict within the organization. They limit their resources, and in so doing, limit the amount that the team as a whole is able to achieve.

Jain also believes that humility works hand-in-hand with inclusiveness. Recall his analogy: "As fruit ripens, its tree starts bending down. This means that as you move up in life, you need to become more humble and more down to earth. You need to point more toward the earth than toward the sky."

Inclusiveness is a leadership characteristic that is often hard to come by. Diversity programs within companies and organizations are only one step. Securing a mix of different types of people is a good start, but true progress is when managers make a diverse mix of people feel included, valued, and important to the overall goals and mission of the organization. Dipak Jain acts as if inclusiveness was a natural and normal thing to do. It should be.

WHY BE INCLUSIVE?

Though families in India are very inclusive, Indian society is segregated. Much of the country still operates under a caste system that separates individuals into different professional and socioeconomic classes. To a large extent, this hierarchy encourages those at the top to look down upon those below.

While Dipak Jain is Indian, he holds the belief that all souls are equal. His last name is derived from Jainism, the religion that he practices, a subset of Hinduism that preaches nonviolence. While his native country still operates under ancient tenets that promote division, Jain advocates a more participatory, transparent, and inclusive organizational structure.

"I come from a culture that is purely hierarchical," Jain says. "And coming from that culture, I feel that hierarchy is wrong because I have seen that style of management lead to more rather than fewer problems. And one thing I learned is that if you are in a hierarchal system, what is important is the people that work with you. They also need to be taken into consideration—they need to have a voice. They have to be a part of the overall decision-making process. Now, you can never reach total consensus, you can never please everyone. If you are soliciting information and you don't do anything with it, you can create more unhappiness. The best organizations create a culture where there is transparency and openness in the system. You promote a sense of fairness and integrity. I have my own personal saying: 'the outcome or the result is the sight, the process of reaching the outcome is the insight.'"

Hierarchies isolate us from each other. They stifle the exchange of ideas and the collective power of teams. The limiting aspect of this rigid structure is not lost on workers. When employees know that there is no system in place for their voices to be heard, what confidence will they have that a leader has all the information necessary to make the best decision?

"The moment you take a hierarchical approach, you have created a problem," Jain explains. " People are not sure whether you are saying what you believe, or saying what you are supposed to because of your position. So, people get confused. Is the message you are sending the real message or the one you think should be delivered?

"If you explain the decision-making process that you went through, then when people see the result, they will buy into it because they know this is how it happened. The process has to be transparent to the system. That is how we need to do things. You don't have to say, I talked to Mr. Smith and not to Mr. Jones; that's not the point. There is a way for people to contribute, to say: 'my ideas and thoughts all went into the decision, my inputs got included, and the output was something that I was a part of.'"

Sadly, exclusion reigns in many workplaces. However, when inclusiveness exists within an organization, individuals feel attached and connected. They know that they belong and play an important role in the growth of their organization. They are involved in shaping the culture in which they work.

HOW IS AN INCLUSIVE CULTURE CREATED?

Many times, culture entails one thing to senior management and something very different to employees. Inclusiveness means to give people a voice. At work, employees should feel that a decision was not a one-person pronouncement. There must be opportunities for group members to listen to others and contribute. Most people need to know that their comments are heard and their contributions are valued. When making a decision, leaders should be able to say: "I listened to everyone; this is what I heard; this is what I am doing; and this is why I am doing it." This creates a culture of inclusiveness.

There are four components for creating inclusive organizational cultures: play the game to "win-win," remember where you came from, harness the human potential, and eliminate complications.

Play the Game to "Win-Win"

Most leaders view business as a zero-sum game. For every winner, there must be a loser. Society celebrates those who are able to secure advantageous deals, even at the expense of others. In boardrooms around the world, you will hear a lot of talk of profits, earnings, and growth. Sadly, thinks Jain, you rarely hear discussion of mutual respect and love.

"My personal values structure is that when I deal with people or organizations, it has to be a win-win scenario," he reveals. "At the end, what you want to be left with is a sense that you are right for each other. After you hire someone, the person should feel very strongly about your organization, and you should feel very strongly about him or her. This is important. I am a big believer in a values system that prevents you from thinking that you got more than the other person. That to me is the start of a problem and not a solution."

Jain recognizes that business deals are not simply about the numbers on the balance sheets. There are people involved and relationships at stake. Decisions are not made in a vacuum, and leaders must be aware of the consequences of their actions.

Remember Where You Came From

Jain was raised in northeast India in the village of Tezpur, where as a child he sat quietly on the floor of his school soaking in the daily lessons. As a graduate student and professor at the remote Gauhati University, he wrote to scholars in the United States to obtain copies of journals and research papers. It was his curiosity and willingness to look beyond his surroundings that eventually brought him to the University of Texas at Dallas to pursue his PhD.

He has lived in America for more than two decades, but Jain returns to southeast Asia often. He values the sense of community and respect for others that exists in Asian cultures.

"We are blessed in one dimension that in the Indian system, we all live together," he says. "We have a joint family system. And I tell you a joint family system is basically an organization. We have four brothers, and they all live together. The father is there, he is the head of the family. We four brothers are like four consultants. There is no hierarchy there. We have our families, we have our children. Each one has to serve its own interest, but we all live together so it becomes like a miniature organization."

The school Jain now heads is a far cry from the crowded, impoverished classroom of his youth. Yet despite his success, Jain always remembers the journey it took for him to arrive at his current position.

"People tend to forget history," he says. "History is an incredibly important thing. You need to know how you arrived here today. How did you reach this outcome? History is where all the insights are. You need to take time and consider what you have done to reach this position. Most of the values we hold, they come from how we were brought up. They come from our parents and our community and we must never forget the influence that they have had on us."

This dichotomy, the need to study the past in order to ensure a better future, is at the heart of effective leadership. It is this willingness to learn, this desire to push forward and tackle new challenges that has served Jain so well.

Dipak Jain still feels very much a part of his family, country, village, school, and faculty. In the same way that he feels very much a part of each these groups, he too tries to make each of them part of him. Inclusiveness is an indispensable watchword for truly effective leaders.

Harness the Human Potential

For a man who operates in a world of acquisitions and accumulation, Jain talks a lot about looking at what we already have.

"I think in business schools we need to have courses that let individuals focus on their inner strengths," Jain suggests. "We have not done a good job harnessing the potential that lies within a human being. And we need to do a good job, because everyone in the world is talented, they have lots to offer but nobody takes the time to dig within themselves. What we all tend to search for and seek out are outward values as opposed to seeing what is already within yourselves."

Jain sees this outward focus as largely self-destructive. Too much energy is spent on jealously, greed, and desire. In looking at others before we look at ourselves, we forsake the gifts that ought to be the easiest and most gratifying to cultivate.

Eliminate Complications

Often leaders try to be all things to all people. There is a perception that they must be experts on everything related to an organization. However, the result is often an individual who knows very little about a lot of things. Jain believes leaders should determine who they serve and focus on delivering for those audiences. This prevents confusion and increases confidence from co-workers.

"I believe strongly that one should lead as simple a life as possible because all the complications that you bring in effect your performance. So, when you say your purpose in life is to do things well, you have moral duties to the different segments of your life you serve. In my case, it's the students, it's my staff, it's my family, and it's my faculty. I need to make sure they feel respected, loved, benefit from my leadership and that I do my best for them. I cannot satisfy everyone, that also I know for sure. However, people should know where I stand and why I do things the way I do."

Jain is not a person that believes in optimization. He says: "I don't go through life saying I want to achieve this, I want to be here, or I want to be there. I have a very simple rule: whatever is given to me, I do it in the best possible manner. Let others be the judge if they want to put me in a particular place. Because once you keep doing things with your whole conscience and with your full effort rewards will be there. So, my mission in life is very simple. I am not a person who believes in too much materialism."

HOW DO YOU PRACTICE INCLUSIVENESS?

The Internet could very well be the most astonishing example of inclusiveness that humankind has ever experienced. Think about it: regardless of color, religion, income, and location, absolutely everyone around the world has access to all information available on the Net. Even more mind-boggling is that everyone has the ability to e-mail and communicate with each other in ways that were never before imaginable or available. The Internet is the ultimate equalizer. No one is judged on appearance or dress. While it offers a unique form of anonymity, it extends a virtual inclusiveness to all. Craigslist is different from other Internet companies. Craig Newmark, founder of the online listings site craigslist, has a vision of community. His team is forever focused on the needs of its members. This sense of inclusiveness is what makes his craigslist.com Web site and company so egalitarian and exceptional.

Craigslist draws over 5 billion page views per month, yet it doesn't spend a cent on marketing. The noncommercial character of the site allows no banner advertising, pop-up ads, or visitor registration. It began as a not-for-profit-seeking community service in 1995, initially listing local cultural events available in the San Francisco Bay Area. Then and now, craigslist acts locally arranging listings city by city for jobs, events, merchandise, real estate, personals, volunteer opportunities, and non-judgmental community discussion forums. Craigslist makes it possible for private parties to get in touch with each other. To make a deal, you are on your own, unlike eBay, where an online sale or transaction is completed with a binding contract. With only 23 employees working from a small office, its low-maintenance operational efficiencies are astonishing. Employees at eBay number almost 9,000.

Caring for his Community

Craig Newmark
Founder of craigslist

Craig Newmark has no arrogance. He works full-time on community or customer service chores. He sits at his computer most every day, and spends his time getting rid of scammers and hackers who attempt to spoil the community he built. He is involved with keeping false advertisers, and potentially illegal and inappropriate posters, off the site. As he puts it, "I do full-time customer service now, but I'll be doing customer service as long as I live. After that, it's probably over. My title just reflects what I do. I'm not a really good manager. I am not as decisive as I should be, and that's a big reason why Jim (Buckmaster) is CEO. He runs things and makes things happy. That works out pretty well. I rely a lot on my experience and intuition, which is to say, my moral compass, and I know when to ask for help."

Newmark finds that by doing customer service, he can follow through on personal commitment, but it also helps him stay in contact with what people really need. If the needs of the customer are truly understood, it enables the employees within a company to stay connected to each other as well as to the customer. The common bond that fuels inclusiveness is the needs and wants of the customer.

"It's more effective sometimes if I'm the one telling the bad guy to cut it out, rather than someone on staff that the bad guy's never heard of," Newmark said. "We just keep plugging away. Customer service can be pretty corrosive when you have to speak to people who are abusive. This is the same thing that happens to a lot of cops when they've been on the job too long."

Inclusiveness pervades his decision making. He often reaches decisions by consulting his community of users. A case in point, he received over 3,000 publicly posted remarks after inviting visitors to share their point of view on charging modest fees to employers when placing job ads in two additional cities (besides San Francisco). Seeking his user community's help again, he sought their input, when he was considering charging apartment brokers for apartment listings in New York City. Trying to be fair to all, brokers and renters alike, his community-reached solution was a modest $10 fee for every broker listing posted.

・・・

Craig's Personal Values

"If you play fair and you work hard, you can get ahead," Newmark says. "I figure you need to make enough money to live okay, and if you can live better, that's okay, but really how much more do you need? And treat people the way you want to be treated. I got these values from my parents and religious school. I became conscious of them back then and, like a lot of people, lost them, but doing craigslist reminded me that we all share those values, and that helped me get them back. My values are not much different than anyone else's; I'm just following through rather than giving the values lip service. A lot of people in a lot of big companies want to do that, but their culture works against that."

He continues: "The values stuff was just implicit when I started craigslist, and I only started thinking about them in the past couple of years and did what felt right, which became my moral compass at the time. I just practice what my values are and keep plugging away, and that became evident in the site as the community expressed more or less the same values, and the values are what attract people to our company. I do realize that we have occasional lapses, so we try really hard to do the right thing all the time."

Newmark says his personal values are continually challenged when people post material that may be against the law. "If something's illegal, we just don't tolerate it," he states. "People in the community tell us that it's illegal. We just don't allow it. Everything we do is up for question; we re-evaluate decisions we've made. Sometimes we change things, sometimes not."

Perhaps without knowing it, Newmark is ensuring that his Web site remains inclusive. By eliminating the "bad guys," he is making it possible for everyone to trust each other on his site. From this sense of trust, people can then not only feel good about interacting with others, but included as well. Inclusiveness can be part of a culture even when you do not actually see the people.

Giving Values a Voice

As to his professional mission: "It's a matter of just following through with my values and giving someone else a break. I would like to change the world, but I'm too lazy, so my plan is to get other people to change the world. We do it in one way just by following through with our values on the site, keeping it almost completely free while providing pretty good customer service. Beyond that, my hobby seems to be working with people in various forms of media, helping media and journalism restore its sense of community service."

According to Newmark, a leader should "pick out values, including the values we all share, and then practice what you preach. The key is to treat other people like you want to be treated. It's more important to practice it than say it; a lot of companies say it and then don't follow through. They follow through half the time but not when it's inconvenient." In the spirit of inclusiveness, Craig Newmark deeply cares for the community he built, gives people a voice, tries to listen thoughtfully, and encourages participation.

Newmark says the following people inspire him: "There are people who are inspirational by sticking their necks out. They blatantly convey their values. For example, Leonard Cohen, Steven Colbert, Jon Stewart, Patrick Fitzgerald. I'm hoping 'Fitzmas' comes soon. It's like Christmas that's provided by Patrick Fitzgerald. Fitzgerald is probably risking his life by doing what he's doing. Colbert is doing the same thing, particularly recently. Leonard Cohen's music is the closest thing I have to prayer. Cohen explicitly addresses issues of spirituality and compassion."

Regarding success, he says, "I don't think about it much. I figure I've acquired significant success spiritually and financially. I've turned down tens of millions of dollars or more, and it just feels right. It didn't feel right to take it, and I'm having more fun this way.

"I'm in a little bit of flux right now. I'm also finding that I have a lot in common with the religious values practiced by the country's founders, for example, George Washington, Thomas Payne, Thomas Jefferson, and Benjamin Franklin, and a form of Christianity that harkens back to the earliest Christians, and the words of Jesus, rather than what followed. The book I just read is called *Faith of the Founding Fathers,* which serves to remind us that what people believed in is very different from what people are telling us these days."

Newmark's most valuable life lesson goes back to October of 1972. He was a sophomore at Case Western Reserve in Cleveland, taking a communications class. "I realized the communications problems I was having couldn't be other people's problems," he remembers. "They had to be mine. I had socialization issues largely related to communication, and that's when I realized they were my problems, not anyone else's. I just was thinking about it; all of a sudden I had an epiphany. It began a process in which I, among other things, started listening to people a lot more. I realized that no matter how good a listener I think I am, I have to be better."

How much better he's become! He now listens to community members or visitors from over 300 cities each month. Inclusiveness, not competition or profit, is craigslist's *raison d'etre*.

ORGANIZATIONAL INCLUSIVENESS

Let's take a look at two other companies that have received awards for their inclusive cultures: Cisco Systems and Whole Foods.

Cisco Systems

As President and CEO of Cisco Systems, John Chambers created a once-a-month breakfast, commonly referred to as Cisco's Birthday Breakfast. During the month of their birthday, employees receive an e-mail from Chambers, inviting them to a birthday get together from 9:00 AM to 10:00 AM. Those who choose to attend, roughly 25 every month, bring questions to ask the CEO. While the birthday celebrants are there for the cake, the real frosting is their spot-on queries about managerial decisions and failings and assessments of corporate strategies. The real purpose of this event is to give everyone an opportunity to voice an opinion about where Cisco Systems is headed.

Chambers puts himself out there. He doesn't hide. Any question is fair game. In fact, he doesn't want the high-profile vice presidents to attend. This event is for the rank and file. He wants open communication, lots of interaction, and candid feedback from employees. In a nutshell, this informal continental breakfast is an effective vehicle for discovering potential problems within a company that is growing at a fast rate. During the breakfast hour he takes from 20 to 50 questions, ranging from "Do you know that we are losing good people in a certain area of the company?" to "Are you concerned that one of our competitors is doing this too?" to "Did you know that potential hires are not experiencing the required five interviews with Cisco employees?" Chambers learns if a gap exists between what's actually happening and what leadership says it is doing. Voted "CEO of the Year" by *Chief Executive Magazine,* the "Best Boss in America" by *20/20,* and the "Best Company in North America and in the World" by *Global Finance,* his inclusive agenda earns positive reviews.

Whole Foods

Whole Foods Market, the world's largest natural and organic foods supermarket, is an inclusive organization. Its Team Members have also rated their company as one of *Fortune* magazine's "100 Best Companies to Work For" for the eighth consecutive year. Three reasons explain employee enthusiasm. Both full- and part-time employees alike receive PPO health coverage; nonexecutives hold 85 percent of the company's stock options; and the company's gain sharing plan adds another 6 percent to employee wages. In fact, Whole Foods is the only national supermarket retailer on the "100 Best Companies to Work For" list and one of only 24 companies to make the list every year since its inception.

John Mackey, Whole Foods Market CEO and co-founder, is quick to point out his original focus when he began the company more than 25 years ago. It was the fundamental importance of Team Member happiness. He believes that the job of the company's leadership is to empower Team Members, and to help them grow, learn, and flourish. As it relates to Team-Member inclusion and empowerment, the year 2003 was an especially spectacular year at Whole Foods. During that year, full- and part-time Team Members were given the opportunity to vote on benefits. These ranged from discounts on items purchased at Whole Foods Market stores to health insurance.

Mackey came up with the idea of employee involvement when he was touring the stores, coast to coast, and listening to their questions and concerns. Employees were asked to share ideas about benefits they would like Whole Foods to offer. After three subsequent votes, the benefit package was finalized. Each employee was given the unique opportunity to get actively involved in the process. Mackey wants to repeat this benefits vote every three years. Whether you call it democracy in action or call it sharing power, these inclusive practices make Whole Foods a great place to work. In 2003, Whole Foods was one of the first U.S. companies to implement a progressive health care program that gives employees a monetary allowance, prompting them to make the kinds of self-empowered health care decisions that directly impact their lives. Inclusiveness produces impressive results.

7

Collaboration

> *"Competition has been shown to be useful up to a certain point and no further, but cooperation, which is the thing we must strive for today, begins where competition leaves off."*
>
> **FRANKLIN ROOSEVELT**

> *"Every aspect of our present well being is due to hard work on the part of others. As we look around us at the buildings we live and work in, the roads we travel, the clothes we wear, or the food we eat, we must acknowledge that all are provided by others. None of these would exist for us to enjoy and make use of were it not for the kindness of so many people unknown to us.*
> *As we contemplate in this manner, our appreciation for others grow, as does our empathy and closeness to them."*
>
> **THE DALAI LAMA in *The Open Heart***

In his sophomore year at Notre Dame, Chris Zorich and his football team were one game away from the National Championship and ranked number one. Their opponent was number-two ranked USC. Notre Dame's starting running back and starting fullback missed curfew. Coach Holtz called a meeting. Chris remembers, "Everybody was looking around like 'Where's Ricky and Tony?' The coach said, 'Our curfew two nights before a game is at 11:00 PM. We had some guys try to get in at 11:30 PM. I sent them home.' We were like, 'You sent home our starting running back and starting fullback? What were you thinking?'" The coach told his players, "This team can win—seniors, take it away from here." Notre Dame won the game.

It is no surprise that Zorich knows what collaboration looks like. To him, it involves working hard and treating everyone equally. "When your football coach treats your starter differently than the third team center, you see it, and all of a sudden you lose respect for that coach," he says. "If the first team linebacker skips curfew and doesn't get in trouble, but the third team linebacker does and he gets sent home, then what message are you sending?"

People have to understand that they are all on the same team. This does not mean that the receptionist is on the same level as the CEO, but everyone should have the same understanding of the mission and overall goals of the organization, buy into them equally, and be similarly committed to deliver them. Before talking about the need to increase profits, management should focus on creating an environment that enables everyone to feel valued and part of the team.

WHAT IS COLLABORATION?

Collaboration means working together. Relationships with others are vital to our success. Alone, our impact is enormously limited. Collaboration means partnership. It involves teamwork, solving tough problems, exchanging insights, sharing knowledge, and communicating frustrations, joys, and victories. It means leveraging people's strengths and recognizing how best to use them towards the good of the organization. Social exchange and cooperative relationships, not isolation and competition, are key to collaboration. It involves creating a mutually beneficial interdependency.

Jerry Fisher, the former VP of Corporate R & D at Baxter Healthcare says, "The best leader I ever worked with is very hands-on in terms of strategies and planning. He takes ownership; it is not just someone else's idea. He simplified the ground rules so that everyone understood the values and was engaged with them. He personally explained each of our principles to everyone in the company either in person and/or by phone. He said, 'This is why it is important to me; this is why it is important to you; this is why it is important to us.' Everything was put in very simple terms in a language anyone could understand."

Collaboration does not work if leaders choose to use others for personal gain. This outdated leadership mind-set sees others as a resource for consumption. Its leaders are interested in acquiring or maintaining power. They believe, 'I have the power, because you don't. If others become self-empowered, then I lose power. It's either them or me.' In this culture, collaboration does not exist. Creating a spirit of collaboration is all about instilling a mind-set where people intrinsically want to help each other succeed, learn, and grow.

••

What Does Collaboration Look Like?

Kimberly Senior
Theatre director and arts educator

Kimberly Senior creates collaboration. As the director of a theatre company and a facilitator of Chicago teen groups, she uses the idea of an "ensemble" in her work. Senior teaches six-week workshops where teens develop and create their own original performance piece. Successful theatre, in her mind, grows out of an ensemble. She describes it as a group of people working together toward a common goal, with a common language, where no individual is greater than the whole; yet, the whole could not exist without the individual components.

"You can't have the whole without all the little pieces that make it up," Senior said. "And not one of the pieces is greater than the sum of its parts. This idea is the most consistent thing in all the work that I do." In creating a theatrical production, she believes the best actor is one that understands what the lighting designer is doing, how the sound designer functions, why the director makes certain choices, and what their partners and team are doing on stage.

Her first step in creating an ensemble is to break down barriers, especially because her teen groups are racially and economically diverse. "Some of the kids I deal with want to be Gary Sinise and other kids don't even know who he is or what theatre is in general, for that matter," Senior comments. "So, to try and find the common language often requires thinking 'Okay, she's a girl. What are your expectations of a girl?' My secret is that I work so fast that they don't have time to be like 'What am I doing here? I don't want to be here. I'm scared. I'm afraid. I'm vulnerable.' It all happens so fast. Often I don't know where the hours go and all of a sudden I'm having fun and I'm connecting to the person next to me. I'm bringing them into the ensemble on the first day."

• •

Between the ages of 14 and 19, the teens have little knowledge of one another, as they come from all over the city. Each group creates a 30-minute original performance piece, whatever they want to make together. Each teen has a voice in creating the piece, whether a painter, singer, dancer, or writer. What happens is powerful. Teens learn tools to be independent, discover their own voice, and create an empowering circle of support.

As Kimberly describes, she is trying to find a point of entry to be able to relate to the teenagers. The basis for all collaboration is discovering similar values, goals, and motivations, and from there, finding common points of interest and intent. Until this is done it becomes difficult to have a meaningful dialogue or work closely as a team. Seeing the bridge that enables people to connect is the framework within which collaboration can evolve.

KEYS TO COLLABORATION

There are six keys to participating individually in a collaborative setting. They are: understand how to relate to each other; don't wear a mask; empower—don't help; toss out perfection; let leaders surface; and carve out mutual relationships. Each serves to build cooperative, mutually beneficial relationships.

Understand How to Relate to Each Other

Finding the link between two people and then among a team of people is the starting point for collaboration. When we are better able to see what motivates another person, we are better able to calibrate how to communicate with them. Each person needs to discover the best forms of communicating interpersonally. Giving each other descriptive praise is another important component of relating; think of it as some lubricating oil that takes the squeaking out of the relationship. It helps to open up the communication channels and foster greater respect between both persons.

Don't Wear a Mask

Kimberly Senior has a style that gets teens to strip away their masks. This is remarkable because teens naturally love to wear them. Senior creates a safe environment for teens to explore by pairing a mentor to each workshop participant. "There is one person who is assigned to me to protect me and guide me and be my pal," one teenager shared. Senior tells her groups that what happens in the room stays in the room, that it is a safe place for them to explore and create an alternate community. She says, "It's not a religious organization; it's not a school; it's not a family. It's creating an alternate structure where there aren't really so many rules about how you have to behave. There aren't hierarchies. There are assumptions right off the bat that everyone's equal. Leaders emerge and different things happen, and that gets dealt with or controlled, or simplified, or evaluated because there are no masks."

If masks are worn, people can never actually connect to each other. It is hard enough to try to effectively communicate to others; it becomes impossible if you are talking to a mask. Unless there is honest, candid, and genuine dialogue between two people, second-guessing and verbal double-talk result.

Empower—Don't Help

There is a thin line between help and empowerment. If a teenager says to you, "I'm pregnant and I don't know what to do," you could get in the car with them, take them to Planned Parenthood, and help them figure things out. This is helping. Alternatively, you could say: "Here's a phone book. Here's how you find the options. Here are the steps that you will need to take to reach a solution." This is empowering. Unlike helping, empowerment stays with them. One of Senior's top values is that you need to stand and walk on your own.

Empowerment has a longer-lasting impact and sets up a problem-solution orientation to the collaboration. Empowering is more beneficial to the team. It is an approach that helps a team flourish, grow, and become stronger and more creative.

Toss Out Perfection

Senior shares another secret: Mentors don't have to be perfect or invulnerable. Once, Senior worked with a group of teenage girls at a neighborhood puppetry theater. One day before rehearsal, Kimberly was standing outside when two dogs attacked her. After she left the hospital, the young girls, who had seen Senior as a capable adult, saw her for the first time as someone who could not walk on her own. For the first time, she needed *their* help. The girls learned that strong people get hurt, too. Senior showed them that everyone sometimes has to ask for support and help.

In fact, showing vulnerability and imperfections, whether personal or physical, are part of developing deeper relationships. These insecurities enable people to be honest with each other, as opposed to supporting a façade of perfection. Collaboration cannot be built on a house of cards. It needs a solid foundation based on truth. To expect and seek perfection gets in the way of relationship building and learning.

Let Leaders Surface

In a collaborative setting, individuals can rise to be a leader in a group. Kimberly Senior discovered this firsthand when she worked with a group of 15 pregnant teenagers. Kimberly would normally call the kids to remind them of Sunday afternoon meetings, but one of the girls rose to the occasion to become the leader. Remarkably, she started calling the other girls to tell them to come to the group. She had assumed a level of self-imposed responsibility she had never experienced before. It gave her life another value. The group of teens challenged Senior's values. She felt there was so much the girls needed to discover about the situation they had gotten themselves into and the choice to have their child. Yet, there were a lot of great things that grew out of that. "I learned a lot from those women," Senior says.

Carve Out Mutual Relationships

The best relationships are mutual. Kimberly asked herself, "How can I expect the kids to learn from me if I'm not opening myself up to what they're teaching me? Kids change and grow. I'm not the expert even though I've worked with over 700 teenagers." She asks teenagers to be themselves with her, to be the best that they can when they are with her. Mentors, parents, and teachers are not perfect, so Senior does not urge young people to try to be like them. Instead, she says, "Be your own self. Be that light in someone's eyes or feel it in your own."

Carving out a mutual "give and take" is possibly the most difficult step of maintaining a relationship. It's one thing to start one, but it is totally different to invest the time and energy required to keep one going. The relationship between two people defines the degree and extent of collaboration.

Being Collaborative

Carol Bernick
CEO of Polished Nickel Capital Management and former Chairman, Alberto-Culver

As the daughter of the founders of Alberto-Culver, the personal health care giant, Carol Bernick's childhood was filled with lessons that could never be learned in a classroom. She was raised by two workaholic parents with seemingly limitless energy from whom she learned the value of commitment. Bernick learned to treat others with respect, regardless of their background. Offered a view from the top at a young age, Bernick learned that success is achieved by having the right people around you, and that leadership is defined by the ability to bring out the best in others. These early lessons have served her well. Now, the chairman of the board and director of Alberto-Culver, she has demonstrated a desire and commitment to collaboration throughout the company.

There are three ways to be collaborative: communicate openly to break the silence, seek people with similar values, and establish an emotional connection.

Break the Silence—Communicate Openly

Bernick did not create herself in the mold of her parents—she built on their experiences. Today, after a 32-year career with the company, she is tasked with bringing it into the 21st century. It is a challenge she does not intend to tackle alone, because she knows success comes from a collegial and collaborative team.

"I spent a life with a family where problems were not discussed, where you pretend that they didn't happen and we hoped that they would go away," she remembers. "I think that's the way many businesses function also. There can be this dead dog lying right there on the table and nobody will address it."

Silence rarely solves anything. Often, one of the most difficult things for an organization to do is admit that it has a problem. However, Bernick learned that apathy and fear of confrontation do nothing except make the problem worse. If there's a dead dog in the room, eventually it begins to smell.

"Deep and thoughtful communication requires a level of emotional intelligence from me and the people that I work with," Bernick says. "I try to seek out people who will communicate and let you get into their psyches, and open up to what they really believe, what they are afraid of, and who they are. People need to know that if there is an issue, we are going to face it; and we can solve anything as long as we talk about it."

Bernick recognizes the power in communicating, the cathartic and empowering potential in the knowledge that one is not alone. Leaders open themselves up and find ways for others to let them in.

Seek People with Similar Values

"Our focus on values isn't a conscious thing; it is a product of who we are and the type of people we hire," Bernick reveals. "Someone mentioned several years ago that we are trying to build a place that you want your kid to work in. We try to get people who identify with the ethics of business and the value of the individual person. I have always believed that you didn't need to give up children or church or community to do a great job at work. I think you have to balance a ton and you have to be a huge and qualified performer. But we would like to go out and find those A-level performers who also want to be A-level in more than one facet of their life."

The easiest way for a business to hold true to its values is to make a concerted effort to hire individuals that embody those principles. Upholding organizational values should never be a compromise someone has to make.

"Personal success for me is making sure that my kids are doing well, are well-adjusted, are enjoying school or their jobs, and are making good judgment calls," she adds. "Parenting is really hard and requires you to check the pulse day-to-day. At work, I know when people are excited; you can sense the passion or the lack of excitement. Success to me is when people are growing and feeling good about what they are doing."

Success in business may be the standard by which the board of directors measures Bernick, but it is not the standard that guides her life. She lives to support and cultivate the people around her and to share values. A values philosophy begins at home and carries over to her company.

Bernick says, "I don't go around saying, 'I'm going to be one of *Fortune*'s most powerful women.' That stuff just doesn't really interest me. I have always just wanted to be in an organization where I made a difference and where I was working with a great group of people whose values I admire."

It's good to ask new recruits and interviewees, "What are your values?" It forces a good discussion on a topic that should be a cornerstone of any selection criteria. Later, those individual's values will help to nurture—or erode—a collaborative spirit among the team.

Establish an Emotional Connection

Bernick remembers, "I read a book once that really resonated with me that said the real purpose of a great leader is to establish an emotional connection that helps other great leaders soar. You have to think about and ask: 'Who is going to lead the leader?' It is not just the rank and file you have to worry about, but how do you unleash the power of the leaders that you have in the building? I don't think there are just ten leaders in our company; there are leaders at all different levels and capacities. The challenge is to make them feel good about turning to other people and getting them engaged." This of course helps to nurture collaboration. It sets up a pattern that says you turn to others to help solve problems—it's not on your shoulders alone. The problem can be shared by the team.

The numbers on a balance sheet will change, the stock price will fluctuate, but an emotional connection will resonate long after the statistics fade. Contrary to popular belief, it is not financial reward that inspires greatness. Leaders find a way to connect with others and inspire the ability each of us has.

"The team is huge. I would never tell you that the team isn't terribly important and I would never say that an individual accomplishes more than a team," Bernick says. "But there are different players that make up the team and I believe you have to touch people individually. I don't think that when I send a note to the entire team it is anywhere near as personal as when I write an individual note."

Establishing an emotional connection is a great way to create sustainable points of contact among team members. These emotional connections set up interpersonal "channels" that link members of a team together—and supercharge common growth and collaboration.

STEPS FOR ACHIEVING COLLABORATION

There are three ways to achieve a spirit of collaboration: let go of pride, get to 90 percent, and have a willingness to gather information.

Let Go of Pride

"With technology, the world is changing more now than ever before. I have come to believe that our critical strength is the ability to look at ourselves and change quickly and not be caught up in the hubris that comes with being a large traditional company," Carol Bernick affirms.

Pride can be a powerful and blinding value. Pride is too often coupled with a misguided confidence, a confidence that assumes that past success ensures future success.

"The best leaders have shown me that it is okay to say you don't know," Bernick shares. "Never be afraid of questions. When you don't know the answer, even if you are supposed to know it, make sure you get back to people. The best leaders I have seen show emotion. They connect with their people. They are not afraid to show them that they are vulnerable."

The collective knowledge of others will always be greater than that of your own. To pretend otherwise or to ignore the input of those around you is ignorant and dangerous.

Get to 90 Percent

"I live with a fear of failure," Bernick confides. "Failure to me is when I screw up or let somebody down. I once had an associate who was underperforming; she didn't have a clue and we had a sales meeting coming up. I ripped into her in front of six or seven of her peers. The team felt terrible, she felt terrible, and I knew I had disappointed all those people who thought highly of me. My personal failures occur when I step outside my values. I value respect more than anything. Yes, she was wrong and doing a lousy job but that was no reason to humiliate her. I disappointed myself and I disappointed everyone on the team. That occurred more than ten years ago and I still think about that mistake."

For Bernick, her greatest failures are not defined by missing sales targets, they are much more personal. They are betrayals of who she is and the values she represents. It is these moments—the rare instances that she steps outside of her values—that haunt her. It is these moments that remind her why her values are the foundation of all her decisions.

"Somebody once shared with me the philosophy that '90 percent is an A' and I think that is a helpful perspective," she comments. "I am always trying to be a perfectionist and that gets me into trouble sometimes. If you look at any friends you have and you pick them apart, you can always find something that you don't like. You just have to remember 90 percent is an A. Now if a person falls in the 60-percent range, I don't have much time for them. In my personal relationships, in dealing with our highest executives, I don't have to agree with everything they do or say as long as we can come to 90-percent agreement."

Mistakes happen. That is important to recognize not only for yourself, but also for those around you. Bernick understands the important thing is not to search for perfection, but rather to search for a shared foundation.

This excellent practice facilitates collaboration. Understanding that no one is perfect and that 90 percent is good enough creates a greater willingness to collaborate. When the leader makes a mistake, forgive and forget it. Everybody is wrong some of the time.

Have a Willingness to Gather Information

Bernick says, "I have worked with some poor leaders before who really don't want to know the facts; they just want to make a decision. So it doesn't really matter what the facts are, it doesn't matter what other people think; they just want it their way. You lose the integrity of the people and the passion of the team when you do that because you are apt to do something that is dead wrong and you won't even listen to the reasons why it is wrong. That is terrible leadership."

It is easy to make a decision, but it is not so easy to make the right one. Some leaders today still operate under a dictatorial mind-set, thinking that those under them will blindly follow orders. However, the power of inclusiveness lies not only in the collective knowledge available to make decisions, but also in the fact that everyone involved has a stake in the success.

"I think the biggest difference between men and women in business is that some men are going to get out there and move forward without gathering," Bernick says. "They don't gather opinions, they don't gather other thoughts, and they don't benchmark much. They hunt. They want to chop down the tree and it doesn't matter if by chopping it down they destroy the world around it. Many women I have seen in executive roles are perhaps more prone to gather more information, gather more opinions. Occasionally, I take some time to make up my mind, but that is often because I have asked for a variety of inputs from people I respect. I may discard some of those opinions, but I value them all. Collaboration is the core of our company."

To bring others in is not a weakness; it is a sign of strength. For a leader not to take advantage of the people they helped assemble, not to take advantage of the talent and resources available to them would be irresponsible.

8

Values-Based Decisiveness

> *"Experience is not what happens to you;*
> *it is what you do with what happens to you."*
> **ALDOUS HUXLEY**

> *"Follow the three R's: respect for self, respect for others,*
> *and responsibility for all your actions."*
> **THE DALAI LAMA**

> *"A teacher affects eternity;*
> *he can never tell where his influence stops."*
> **HENRY ADAMS**

Several years ago, Galeta Clayton, founder and headmistress of the Chicago City Day School, faced the decision of whether or not to offer half- or full-day kindergarten classes. It was an issue of great contention among parents and one that was sure to cause anger and frustration, no matter the outcome. "It would have been easy to compromise our values, pander to the marketplace, and extend the day to satisfy working parents' needs," remembers Clayton.

"Yes, it was tough. It took the teachers, however, only a short period of time to decide: half-day classes only," she continues. "They just said what they thought was in the best interest of the kids. They knew that at such a young age, a full day was too long for four- and five-year-olds. So professionally, I think we always ask ourselves, when something tough comes up, or we have a personal issue or whatever, 'Is it in the best interest of the kids or not?' If we can say yes to that, then we've made the right decision."

Values can be a powerful lens through which individuals can make important decisions. For Clayton and her staff, providing the best environment for the children is the yardstick by which everything else is decided and measured.

"I think that values are something you have to live," Clayton said. "When they become a part of you, there isn't a conscious decision; you don't have to ask if you are behaving in an ethical way or 'Am I living what I preach?' When you mature, your values are so firmly entrenched it is tough to change them."

Values have the power to shift our decision-making into automatic mode. They set up a framework against which decisions are made, checked, and confirmed. Values inform decisions.

WHAT IS VALUES-BASED DECISIVENESS?

Making decisions is hard. There is always the risk of failure, ridicule, or negative consequences. That is why leaders are often indecisive. They put decisions off and wait until they are made by default; the time period passes, the opportunity goes away, or the candidate takes another job. Decision-making requires courage to make tough decisions, to know when to stop assessing and make a yes-or-no call.

A distinguishing characteristic of a good leader is the ability to make informed decisions in a timely way. However the historical backdrop that characteristically describes decision-making is a tough-minded, strong-willed, quick-to-act person, who is critical and firm.

A values-based decision maker is vastly different. Using intuition, judgment, experience, as well as informed input from others, this leader uses values to serve as a filter in the decision-making process. Holding true to them makes decision-making easy.

What Does Values-Based Decision-Making Look Like?

Galeta Kaar Clayton
Founder and Headmistress,
Chicago City Day School

Galeta Clayton sees the future. She sees it in the children that walk the halls of the Chicago City Day School, the independent elementary school that she founded 25 years ago. Clayton sees the children of today, and she worries. She worries that we ignore the uniqueness of each child. She worries that we are concerned more with process and politics than we are about love. She worries that we are churning out individuals who don't understand the meaning of trust and respect.

The daughter of two teachers, Clayton grew up recognizing the importance of education in shaping values. She has taught in public and private schools, urban neighborhoods and suburbs, and nearly every grade. Yet her enthusiasm for her work and the potential she sees in today's youth remains as strong as when she first became a teacher nearly 40 years ago.

"Whether you are in a large school, small school, public, or private, I think what you have to have in order to be successful is a passionate, unalterable belief that all kids can learn," she says. "You have to understand that people learn differently and everyone has a different capacity for learning and that we need to respect that diversity."

These are Clayton's core values. They inform and guide her decision-making on a daily basis at the school.

Decisiveness is often challenging when you have other people assist in the decision-making process, such as customers, clients, members, or, in the case of a school, parents. As Clayton says, "Parents often believe they should be making the decisions in the school since their child attends there. But I don't think that everybody who goes up to the bank teller to cash a check should be making decisions to help run the bank. Educational decisions are so intricate and weighty—they need to be made by educators."

Abandoning the Competitive Mindset

Clayton was adopted. The only child of two loving parents to whom she was the center of the universe, she was never hungry as a child and never wanted for anything.

"I think very often about the accident of birth," she shares. "Adopted children always think about the accident of birth, probably more than a child who just appears in a family. You are so much more aware of what your life could have been and how fortunate you are, so maybe my collegial cooperative sense comes from that."

As a child, Clayton did not have to fight with siblings for attention. She never competed with brothers or sisters to see who received higher grades in school or scored more points in a game. However, if Clayton wanted to share, if she wanted to spend time with others, she had to make the first gesture. While other people were struggling to keep people away, Clayton developed the ability to bring individuals closer.

"I am very careful in how we treat people," she says. "I would never knowingly hurt somebody. I think civility and courtesy are just sort of a way of life. I see road rage, and I think to myself that I wouldn't even know how to make those gestures at people. I am sure you see it in a competitive workplace. Maybe a part of it is that my personal and professional values do not include competition, but sometimes it exists in a business workplace."

Society accepts the idea that business is inherently competitive, that we should value leaders who are cutthroat and will do anything to get to the top. Clayton understands, however, that the only thing that happens when you claw your way to the top is that all the people you injured on the way up will try to tear you down.

"There is an idea that in order to be successful in business, you have to be aggressive, that you cannot be mutually respectful and supportive," she says. "People begin to internalize that 'ideal,' and feel like they have to compete or keep up with everyone around them. It becomes a part of who they are."

Too often individuals measure themselves not against their own potential, but against the achievements of others. Great leaders recognize that the most powerful motivation comes not from beating those around you, but rather in achieving the goals you have set for yourself. Clayton places cooperation at the top of her values list. It serves as a filter for her educational decision-making at the school.

WHAT ARE THE BENEFITS OF DECISIVENESS?

There are individuals that show up to work, but are never truly there. They are disengaged and distant. They give minimal effort and count the minutes until the workday ends. They believe that regardless of their effort, they will receive little in return.

"As a leader, you have to create a caring community," Clayton says. "That is the basis for everything else. If you have not brought people closer together, if you have not trusted, respected, and encouraged the team, respected and rewarded the words of the individual and nurtured them, then you have nothing. You have to say loud and clear that we all care about each other."

A community does not form naturally. Rather it must be cultivated through a sense of openness and importance. People have to want to join a community; they must recognize that by being part of a group they will achieve more than what they could accomplish alone.

"I don't think leaders have to be friends with the people that they work with, but they do have to make the work meaningful," Clayton reveals. "The way you make work meaningful is to trust, respect, and value those around you."

Too often leaders confuse friendliness with respect. Respect requires that you trust that your team will uphold the value of the organization. Respect involves more than compliments and a smile. Respect requires that you reward those around you who have earned it. Great leaders command respect because that is what they offer to those around them.

Instilling Real Authority

Many leaders in business monopolize the decision-making power in an organization. They insist on controlling everything and paralyze those around them. This selfishness weakens the organization and limits the ability to utilize the great resources other team members possess.

Clayton states, "The decisions that people in our organization make are real. We don't have governing structures that are a mockery. I never ask for someone's opinion on something that I am not going to follow through on."

Great leaders recognize that counting on those around them is a sign of strength and not weakness. Even worse than a dictatorial approach is one that offers the appearance of shared authority only to then usurp that power from people later on.

"There are few things that will alienate people more than when they feel their authority is undermined. You can't have just the appearance of independence and inclusiveness, you actually have to demonstrate that you respect others," says Clayton. She is so right.

Building Stronger Links with Values

Effective leaders recognize that everyone on a team plays a role; everyone is there for a reason. Working together inherently bonds people together, for better or worse, and the larger group will feel the actions of a few. Shared values are essential for the team. They unite everyone in the group and guide the decision-making process at each turn.

When great leaders develop teams, they are not just assembling the right skills and backgrounds; they are determining the right people. It is easy to look at countless resumes and numbers and forget that what truly matters is the individual person and the values of that individual. A skill is generally replaceable, but each member of a team is going to be unique.

"I don't think that you can have a strong organization, if you don't have a sense of teamwork," shares Clayton. "In the small organizations where I've worked in the past, the impact of an inappropriate individual—whether inappropriate for the institution or the team—has been felt pretty strongly. So maybe you are only as strong as your weakest links—and you need a strong team to survive."

There is no such thing as a meaningless job in an organization and, as such, a leader should never be nonchalant about selecting a team member. People decisions are among the most important decisions that a leader has to make. Clayton knows that the most effective way to select a team member is to look to the values of the organization, what the school as a whole stands for. By using those values, she usually is able to make the right decision.

"We are very careful with people in my organization," says Clayton. "We are careful about hiring, because we give our teachers a lot of autonomy. We have shared values about how we feel about kids and about where we want to get them in the educational process, but individuals are given a lot of flexibility in terms of accomplishing those goals. I think their ideas are really respected."

Standing Your Ground

A couple of years ago Clayton had parents remove their child from the school. They were a wonderful family that had been enrolled in the school for years. However, Clayton absolutely refused to put this child in a math group in which he did not belong. She explained that although they would do almost anything to please them, it was not in the best interest of the child, and so they wouldn't do it.

"It would have been easy to compromise on what the faculty felt was in the best interest of this child and cater to the parents' wishes to put him in the advanced math group, but that really would have been wrong for the child," Clayton insists.

Individuals today are all too willing to take the easy way, to make exceptions. However, the result is that a series of compromises reaches the point where values no longer have any meaning. Using the shared values of the organization to guide decisions is vitally important. All too often, political correctness replaces values-based decision-making.

"Political correctness has been raised to an art form, and that is bad thinking," continues Clayton. "I think it is a form of moral relativism, the idea that because it is happening, makes it okay. It is really confusing to teachers and to kids. We need to be a holdout against that kind of thinking."

Instead of promoting respect, political correctness actually ignores the individuality that makes each of us special. Instead of helping individuals move ahead, it holds people back as a group. Even worse, political correctness is used as an excuse for eroding our values.

"The pedagogy is one thing, but it is not a real challenge to our values. The other stuff, when we look the other way and make excuses, that is the harmful stuff, like if we say plagiarism isn't bad, and its okay if he cheated a little bit," clarifies Clayton. She is spot on. Ill-fated decisions, like rationalizing cheating, occur when values erosion creeps in and eventually becomes pervasive.

HOW DO YOU PRACTICE VALUES-BASED DECISIVENESS?

A leader should be the face and voice of an organization.

"The tone of an organization all comes from the top," Clayton says. "I can't think of a single time since we started our school when morale has been a problem, and I think that's kind of amazing. I don't mean that from time to time we haven't had somebody who stirs the pot or something, but we just take the stance that you are not going to work here and poison this pot. We are absolutely not going to have it."

Leaders stand by those around them who are willing to uphold the values of the organization. They have to make it clear that membership on that team means something significant.

"When I hire someone to join our organization, I take on a certain amount of responsibility for that person. I defend them when I can and set them up to succeed," Clayton shares. "But as part of that, I am not willing to accommodate dissatisfied people. The time to stop accommodating others is when they lose sight of what makes the organization great."

Valuing team members does not mean that you bend over backwards for them. Rather, the best way to honor the organization is to stand by the values that guide everyone's behavior. As the leader of the organization, it is important to continually make decisions based on these values. To deviate would be a disservice to both the individual and what the team as a whole stands for.

Staying Young among the Children

"I believe," says Clayton, "in the unlimited potential of people to be good, to be trustworthy, and to be able to grow and change. I have seen it in my own professional life and how different I am now than I was when I started teaching. You can't just grow old, not change, and die on the vine. You need to keep growing and stay young, and the kids do that for me."

Those who are content with who they are and refuse to change will be left behind by those around them. Times change, and leaders would be well-served by looking ahead at where they can go instead of merely focusing on where they are.

"One of my favorite books, when I taught English, was *To Kill a Mockingbird*. I reread the book recently. It is just a simple little book that says a lot about leadership and about an unwavering commitment to honesty and clear thinking. It speaks to the wonderful ability that very young children have to cut through the pretense and phoniness and see what people are really about. That is such a wonderful quality."

Often individuals make things more complicated than they need to be. They are worried about myriad consequences and countless decisions they have to make. Often, the simple view of a child can be a powerful tool. Is it right or wrong? Sometimes a decision is that easy.

Hoping for the Future

A lifetime educator, Clayton balances her worry over the state of schools today with her belief in the strength of our children. The leaders of today may fall short of our expectations, but the leaders of tomorrow walk the halls of her school and their future has yet to be written.

She concludes, "Our little school's most practical hope for impact is to turn out youngsters who are compassionate, concerned, humane people, who will assume leadership positions in the world. I don't think the Chicago City Day School is going to save mankind, but unless the notion that children are precious and need to be cared for and liked becomes pervasive in our schools, I don't know what is going to happen."

Leaders with Clayton's strength of character, dedication to community, caring leadership style, and adherence to values create a loving place to nurture the future.

•••

Finding Value with Values

Randy Larrimore
Retired CEO of
United Stationers

"To live your life, you have to have a set of values or something that you stand for. I don't know how you manage if you don't have a sense of values from which to base how you operate. It's the guiding light that takes you through the day and is who you are," exclaims Randy Larrimore.

When he became CEO of United Stationers, he gathered his management team together for a three-day session to discuss the future of the company. The newly appointed Fortune 500 leader stepped on stage before a crowd anxious to learn his vision for success. What they heard was Larrimore paraphrasing from Dr. Seuss's book, *Oh the Places You'll Go:* "Today is our day. We're off to Great Places! We're off and away! There is fun to be done! There are points to be scored. There are games to be won. Our mountain is waiting. So let's get on our way!" By reading this book, he expressed his values to the group, albeit in a very creative way. He wanted the group to have fun, work hard, and win the game together.

For Larrimore, values are not rhetorical devices or convenient symbols; values are at the center of any successful business model. "If you have happy associates, they are more likely to better satisfy your customers, who are more likely to develop loyalty to your company and buy more of your product or service," he says. "This will also make the employees happier. I think shareholder value can be driven by a strong set of values within an organization. If you are going to empower people and push decision-making down, and give people a sense of responsibility, then you have to have a strong set of values—so that you are confident they are going to make the decisions that will benefit the company overall."

Unquestionably, Larrimore finds value in values. They permeate, guide, and inform decision-making—everywhere within his company.

Living "The Golden Rule"

In a business world feared for its complexity, Randy Larrimore operates according to one simple rule—The Golden Rule.

"My personal values are based around treating other people as I would like to be treated," he says. "Everything is based around that. That leads to treating people with dignity and respect no matter what their station in life. I think it also leads to a strong belief in honesty and integrity."

In college, Larrimore worked for DuPont as a computer programmer. Normally, engineers would turn in their programs at the end of business and they would be run by overnight operators and returned sometime the next day. However, Larrimore's results would frequently come back first thing the following morning and sometimes even that business day. While his colleagues were waiting around, Larrimore was able to be twice as productive.

He remembers, "I was asked by a couple of the engineers how I got such turnaround. I thought about it a bit and I realized I think that it came from the fact that I went over and talked to the people in the computer room. I learned that John bowled on Tuesday night so I would ask him about his bowling on Wednesday and that Mary had a kid in college and I would talk about that. While I was standing around, I would simply just talk with them as people and I think they responded to that. I hadn't thought about it at the time, but later I realized that I must be getting that kind of service because when my name came up in the queue they knew me and somebody would say, 'Why don't I run Randy's program first.'"

Too often we treat people based on perceived differences without taking the time to see our similarities. We ascribe individuals certain traits based on job position, gender, race, and ethnicity, and treat them accordingly. Businesses with traditional hierarchal structures support this divisive ideology.

However, at the end of the day, we are defined and united by far more than what can be seen on the surface. Effective leaders are able to look beyond the superficial and connect with individuals in a significant, yet often incredibly simple way. Larrimore puts treating people with dignity and respect at the top of his values list. The Golden Rule serves as a filter for his actions and decision-making in his company.

Relating to Others

Larrimore's grandfather grew up in a small Delaware town of around 8,000 people. When he was about 11 years old, his father died and he had to drop out of school to support his family. As the oldest of five children, Larrimore's grandfather took whatever position he could find to provide food for his brothers and sisters.

As he moved from job to job, he learned how to relate to people of all backgrounds. He made friends everywhere he went, impressing people with his work ethic and inviting personality. Even walking down the sidewalk in the evening, he would make a point to say hello to everyone he passed. It is this ability to connect with others that he passed on to his son, who passed it on to his son.

Larrimore remembers, "I never even realized that there were any religious differences until I got into college because my parents treated people of various religions the same. It just never crossed my mind that if you were Catholic or Jewish or something else, that it mattered.

So I think this whole notion of respecting others and not really caring about their background came from my parents."

Before college, Larrimore worked during the summers at an ice plant. Most of the other employees were African-American men in their 50s who had never attended college. Even many years after Randy had left for school, every time his father would go by the plant, the workers would ask about Randy.

"Despite all I've accomplished, my father has said a number of times that one of the things he is most proud of is that when he returns to the ice plant, they ask him about his son," he says. Without a doubt, Larrimore values relating to others, just like his grandfather before him. It is a value that has shaped his personal and professional life, and guided his decision-making throughout his career.

Talking through the Tough Times

"I think that your values are always challenged, certainly at work when you are trying to make personnel decisions," Larrimore says. "We went through a restructuring where we ended up laying off a lot of people. One of the things I tried to communicate was that respecting people and having strong values doesn't mean that you can't demand performance. People get confused about that. They sometimes walk away from a discussion about treating people with respect and dignity thinking that, 'I can't fire anybody' or 'I can't be demanding from a performance sense.' My response is that it's better to communicate openly and honestly than to try to hang on to them for two or three years because you haven't been completely honest in your performance reviews."

Honesty is not always easy. Subscribing to strong values does not mean you allow inferior performance. To truly respect an individual and an organization is to strive for excellence and to make necessary changes when that level of performance is not met.

Larrimore shares, "In our restructuring, we decided in advance that we had to let people go. We did it in a way that upheld our values. We offered people the opportunity to voluntarily resign, and gave them an extra 50-percent increase in their severance benefits. It was amazing how many people really had something else they wanted to do in life. We were able to offer people protection for a period of months, which allowed them to go back to school or take time to find a new job. We ended up having two-thirds of the necessary layoffs come from voluntary resignations. The end result was that we had no legal action brought against us, not even a hint of unfairness in the way we went about our restructuring. We provided counseling; we provided outplacement services."

Effective leaders do not abandon their values in the face of adversity; they use them to guide their actions and decision-making. This perspective provides individuals and organizations with the fortitude to weather occasional setbacks, knowing that they have a foundation that everyone can believe in and count on.

Coveting Success, Not Power

Being a leader does not mean you are at the top looking down. It does not mean that you exercise control over those who work with you and wield power over them. Fear is a tool that motivates an individual to do just enough to avoid consequences. Shared success is a goal everyone will strive for.

"Unfortunately, I think the world is full of people that care more about themselves than about the company or the people within the company," Larrimore contends. "It is important for me to make high-level decisions, but the company can't succeed unless the receptionist is doing her job as well. People will find me running the photocopier at night or when I am getting ready for a board meeting. At that moment, it is more important that my secretary is doing her typing, and if I have to photocopy that is fine. We do recycling around here and people catch me carrying my recycling bin and dumping it like everybody else. They seem to feel that that's odd, but it's not. Why should I ask somebody else to do it?"

Success is a by-product of everyone doing his part. No one is above or below doing what is best for the team.

Larrimore wants to build deep and meaningful two-way relationships, convey trust and respect, and express loyalty and love. These values were the ones he stressed when he selected the Dr. Seuss book to read to his employees. They guide his decisions, and in the words of Seuss, define "the places you'll go!" Adhering to core values makes you "the winning-est winner of all."

II

Activating
— THE —
Seven Steps to Change

Step 1—Reach Out to Serve Others

> "I expect to pass through this world but once.
> Any good therefore that I can do, or any kindness
> or abilities that I can show to any fellow creature,
> let me do it now. Let me not defer it or neglect it,
> for I shall not pass this way again."
>
> **WILLIAM PENN**

> "Too often we underestimate the power of a touch,
> a smile, a kind word, a listening ear,
> an honest compliment, or the smallest act of caring,
> all of which have the potential to turn a life around."
>
> **LEO BUSCAGLIA**

If we want to change our organizations and shape a new definition of success, then a bold first step is mandated.

Our first step is: Reach out and serve others.

Did you expect this step to be first? Probably not—it might feel counterintuitive to most readers because we tend to think from the inside out rather than the outside in. The road to success has as much to do with others as it does with you.

You might ask: What does reaching out to serve others have to do with individual and organizational success? A service-oriented mind-set creates an open, giving, and collaborative attitude and culture. By any standards, these qualities produce qualitatively happier individuals and a more productive work environment. Giving to others magnifies our hearts in ways that loosen us up to better communicate, interact with, and understand others. This has a profound impact.

We must transcend the internal confines of our workplace and expand the parameters of our focus into our home, community, and the globe. When we do, our other-directed thinking creates a culture so empowering that we receive benefits in return. In any form—caring for the sick, improving schools, focusing on environmental and energy issues, or helping people in developing countries—service requires money, brains, and time. However, making a commitment to service is the key.

We saw a glimpse of this other-directedness in the United States after 9/11. A kindred spirit bonded Americans together and we became one group reaching out to help victims, their families, and each other. Adversity provided a national sense of community that has faded since that tragic event. When we choose to serve, we can change the dynamics of our office, home, school, community, nation, and world. While it sounds like an impossible goal, we believe it is absolutely attainable.

WHY FOCUS ON SERVICE?

So, why launch a discussion on the seven steps to change with service outside of the organization itself? Because by giving time, dollars, expertise, ideas, advice, and sheer brawn, we create a giving environment. It is an environment that is not just self-centered, but rather one that is also intended to serve consumers and employees first. Within the business world, one often hears, "The purpose of a corporation is to increase shareholder wealth." What a crock! We strongly feel: The purpose of a corporation should be to create products and services that satisfy consumer and customer needs in a way that enables employees to feel proud of where they work and reward shareholders with profits and increased stock price. The focus here is on the quality of goods and services produced instead of the size of the profits made.

The new mantra is: Leave a legacy of giving; make charity a major part of your life; take your gifts—personal and professional—and enrich your job, family, and community; make a substantial difference and do as much as you can for others. This is how the world improves. Just as Gandhi taught us, *be the change* that we wish to see in the world, and encourage others to do the same.

There is an old Indian proverb that says, "Everything that is not given is forever lost." When we help others find ways to be of service to their co-workers, friends, family, and the larger community, we help them see the value of dedicating a portion of their lives to a larger purpose. Acts of kindness and service always help the giver as well as the receiver—and they are never lost.

On the work front, show kindness to your colleagues. Insist that co-workers treat each other with kindness, too. Discuss with others what it means to be kind. Look for ways to show kindness to another person who may be especially needy, maybe someone who has received bad news or is troubled. Talk to others about the members of your team. Is there anyone who needs a kind thought or act? How about the person who is "different"? How about the colleague who is difficult or mean? Even if one does not feel like being kind, there is value in doing it anyway because the kind act itself can change one's feelings.

A giving mind-set says: Let me try to make the world a better place. It can include picking up trash, or helping musicians or younger actors just starting out in theater, like Susan Anton—or speaking one's mind about a controversial topic or spearheading a campaign offering food and shelter to the homeless in a developing country, like Paulette Cole.

"God Don't Make Junk"

Susan Anton
Broadway star, actress, and recording artist

It is easy to find Susan Anton after one of her headlining performances in Las Vegas. The actress and singer is not backstage sipping champagne in her private dressing room or signing autographs for her fans—although they often wait for her after the show—or riding in a limousine back to her suite.

Instead, the Hollywood star is picking up trash that patrons have left on the floor outside the theater.

Most people know Susan Anton as a stunningly beautiful woman with a melodic voice. They know her from her roles on television, movies, and the stage as a talented, versatile performer.

Susan Anton sees herself as a trash collector. She believes that is what God has asked her to do.

MEETING EACH OTHER'S NEEDS

One of Anton's favorite Bible passages says, "Wives, honor your husbands and make sure all his needs are met." It is followed by the sentence, "Husbands honor your wives and make sure all her needs are met."

So often we are focused on what we want to the exclusion of others. We think the only way to find success is to cling to our own goals.

Anton says, "My husband and I have a deal: whoever can give up on their position fastest is the winner. Because who needs a position? I know what I know, but I want to understand what he is thinking and feeling. It has completely taken our relationship to a new, deep, and beautiful level."

Anton recognizes the value when you open yourself up to others. Instead of taking something away, that attitude of inclusiveness makes her relationships more meaningful and, in turn, makes her a stronger individual.

"I realized that the more that I focused on my husband's needs—and not in a way where I am sacrificing, but where he understands that he is needed and that he is valued—we can create a situation where we realize how much we need each other," she says. "From that way of thinking, if we are both giving that to each other, we are able to elevate ourselves together."

THROWING OUT THE DOLLAR SIGN

Anton has been working with the same band for more than 25 years. They have stayed together through countless obstacles—divorce, death, children, and financial troubles. These six men became Anton's second family.

There were times over the years when money was short. Anton had offers for work, but it would have meant abandoning her band. For her, it was never worth it. The 25 years of loyalty was worth far more than a single paycheck.

"You have to throw the budget out of the equation here—we are talking about people," Anton states. "This isn't about money. You can get the dollar sign out of the way, and that will take you further down the road than you could ever imagine. But you don't know where the road goes; you just have to trust that it'll take you where you need to go."

When you make choices based on money, it becomes too easy to ignore people. Money can't buy loyalty or love or family. Relationships aren't built on money; they are built on respect for others.

"I have never made my choices based on money or whether it was a career move," she reveals. "I don't make my decisions based on how they would be perceived by others. I have had a lot of people tell me that this or that is a bad decision—that I've been headlining and I can't do an opening act, for instance. But I know when it feels right in my heart, and then I can make the decision. Knowing whether I feel it in my heart . . . it is like a tuning fork. There is a certain vibration when you know your heart is moving you."

Years ago, Anton was performing in a four-week show in a Las Vegas hotel. The hotel had made a big investment in the act, but ticket sales were slow during the first couple of weeks. Anton could see that things were improving and hated to leave just as the show was starting to show a profit. She decided she would continue to perform for free beyond a month as long as the hotel agreed to take care of the musicians.

For the next four weeks, the show completely sold out. The hotel had faith in her and she decided to repay them. She could have taken her salary and left after her four-week run. Instead, she created a partnership that helped the musicians, the hotel, and her own career.

HONORING FAMILY

Anton's love of family developed from her own parents. She watched how they learned from each other.

"My dad was an only child," she remembers. "He never really knew his father and his mother died when he was young. My mother came from a big family—four girls including herself. She had a challenging father who she wasn't very close with, but a caring mother. She got from my father the caring that she never got from her own father. My father got from my mother the family he never had growing up. What I got from them both was the value of family, and that is how I move forward in my own life. But there are so many families that I am a part of: my personal family, co-workers, and the family of man. Being part of that family is part of the point of our existence here."

Family can be more than blood. Family are individuals for whom you sacrifice, the individuals who you care for the way you care for yourself. Providing for family is not an obligation; it is an honor.

"My mother always worked at whatever job she needed to do, and my father worked two jobs in order for the children to be provided for," she says. "It was never about them—it was always about the children and the family. I never once heard my father complain. He just accepted it as his lot in life that he was always working two to three jobs."

LIVING AS A SERVANT

Anton says, "I am a servant—and I say that with great pride. The man who clears your table at the restaurant, he is greater than the person who owns the place. He is in service. I want to be in a position where I can find a need, and I can serve it. I am most joyful when I am in service to others. I love being able to take care of other people. My purpose is to be as aware as possible about how I can serve the people, the situation, the Earth. It goes back to the trash thing—you pick it up. Or when you see someone in need, a mother in the parking lot with her hands full of groceries, you help her. You help people; you are in service to them, whenever you can."

Anton went through a period of time when she didn't take many jobs. None of the offers she received felt right and she didn't want to work just for the money. Eventually, an offer came for a musical in Las Vegas that seemed perfect. However, Anton learned that they were going to cut all of her musical pieces.

A singer by trade, she was worried that the role was not right for her. Slowly, it became apparent that it was not about showcasing her talents. Instead Anton began to see how her role could help others.

"I realized that this is actually about humility, and about service," she says. "There was a greater purpose for me in this play than getting out there and saying, look at what I can do. This was about being humble and not letting my ego dominate. This was about service to the company. There were so many kids in the show just starting out, and this was about helping them and being a leader for them."

Just like in the corporate world, egos play a big role in show business. There is a tendency for individuals to crave the spotlight. Yet effective leaders recognize that often the greatest returns come when you play a supporting role and let others shine. Service is not about subjugating yourself to others; it is about offering your talents for a greater end result for all.

IGNORING THE CRITICS

There will always be critics, individuals who focus on our faults and tell us why we will fail. Pointing out everything that is wrong is easier than working to make it right.

Anton reveals, "I've learned to not need others to tell me that I am good, that I am worthy, or that I belong. The nice thing about getting older is that now I see the value isn't there. It is about the beauty that is inside you. The biggest transformation for me is that it is no longer about me. It is about being in a situation where I can have a positive affect on someone or something."

Great leaders don't need external approval and validation to tell them they are right. They are driven by their own conviction. They know that it is not about what is written in the newspapers, or said on television. It is about what they feel within themselves and how they provide for others.

"Two critics can come to the same exact show and sit right next to each other and see something completely different," she explains. "You'll go crazy if you live according to that, trying to satisfy both of them. So I have to ask myself on a daily basis whether I am serving myself or someone else—my family."

DEFINING SUCCESS FOR YOURSELF

Most business leaders measure success financially; profits, revenues, and stock price are what matters, but that is never enough. Your gains always have to be higher than your peers; next year has to be better than the one before. These external standards create an ever-demanding cycle for success. Anton sees a similar point of view in her profession.

"Defining success in the entertainment business is tough because you are only successful based on who or what you are compared to," she says. "But I was taught not to compare and not to set your standards based on others. That isn't how you measure success. I can't think that someone has a better home just because it looks nice on the outside. I don't know what is going on inside, or whether I would want to live there. Professionally it is really easy to fall prey and feel like a total loser. The industry loves to build you up, tear you down, and then 'find' you again. It is always about something external, but the truth is that all the best things come from inside. It is just a big business, and as long as we honor the dollar more than we honor the spirit, we are going to have to deal with this."

This externally focused mind-set considers only what one can get out of a situation and forgets what a person gives. However Anton, like other great leaders, recognizes the importance of bringing people together for a common goal, not dividing them. There is tremendous power in unity and inclusiveness.

"I am a child of the 60s, so the Beatles are my heroes forever and ever," Anton says. "They changed the world and they made songs for the people who were against war and about love. With them, it was about coming together. We spoke up then, and we used art, music, and films to catch people's attention. There was a social consciousness to the art that was being created."

CUTTING OUT THE BULLSHIT

No profession is filled with more empty promises and falsities than show business. Gossip is commonplace, scandal is routine, and backstabbing is the norm. This atmosphere makes for entertainment and intrigue, but it does not create a healthy work environment.

"Show biz and bullshit are almost synonymous," Anton says. "I heard a saying I thought was cute: 'I don't mind you pissing on me, just don't tell me it's raining.' If I have to work on something, tell me in a nice constructive way what I have to do. Don't keep quiet in front of me and then behind my back say something hurtful. There is only room for so many of us, so we have to hold each other up and support each other."

In a profession filled with individuals vying for stardom, Anton believes in the value of teams. As one of five children, she realized the benefits of having different points of view. Like other great leaders, she understands that diversity breeds strength.

"If you take a little twig, it is fragile, and it can easily snap. But, if you tie 20 twigs together, all of a sudden it isn't so fragile and it doesn't snap so easily," she explains. "I can't go on stage without my band. If I go on stage as 'the star' I am in trouble. I can't go onstage without help. You have to lead with your best intentions and best character, and you have to be impeccable in your character, but it is always about the team that you are leading, and doing the things that you think are best for the team."

In the 1980s, Anton performed as the opening act for George Burns. Each night when she took the stage Burns would look in from the wings and cheer her on.

Years earlier, she was opening for Sammy Davis Jr. in Las Vegas. One night he came into the dressing room and gave her some advice, "Give them everything you've got, do the best you can, and remember that they didn't come to see you anyway." Months later, when Anton was headlining, Davis Jr. sat in the lighting booth to make sure the spotlight shown on Anton the right way.

It is that type of selflessness and positive attitude that Anton looks to share with her colleagues.

• •

Caring for Causes

Paulette Cole
CEO and Creative Director of ABC Home and ABC Home & Planet Foundation

Paulette Cole is caring, creative, compassionate, and completely cause-focused. She is a bright star on a dark night, navigating not only her customers to hearth and home, but also to her social concerns. She wants to help people express their values through their purchases and have their homes become sacred spaces. As the CEO and creative director of ABC Home, her leadership style is incomparable, a model for industry and consumers alike.

In 2005, her ABC Home Manhattan store, which sells everything from chairs and carpets to chocolates, earned almost $80 million in sales.

Each week, some 22,000 customers visit her store. She believes that all things stem from the creative direction of the company. "I want to set the paradigm that creativity should be most valued and rise to the top of the pyramid," she says. "When the bottom line is at the top of the pyramid, something really isn't right. You are just results-driven, but I believe in being creatively-driven, which ultimately yields results."

Cole says intuition strengthens leadership. Social issues are the essence of her company and its success. More leaders should turn up their intuitive volume and follow her example.

"The store is really about representing products from all over the world. We have developed standards for fair labor, recycling, and sustainability," she says. "Since we've started this mission, 20 percent of our inventory is now cause-related. It is either sustainable, from a cooperative, or it is to maintain an indigenous design." Her goal is to increase this to 100-percent responsible design that is environmentally and socially conscious. Her company is now in a position to create this demand.

• •

However her commitment to social causes also extends to her ABC Home & Planet Foundation, where gifts can be purchased in honor of a friend or loved one. It allows one of her selected organizations to provide a service or good to a needy community or developing country. Available for purchase are: one-third share of a "kid" or goat for $40, one-third share of a water buffalo for $50, entrepreneurial training for $125, the safe birth of a Tibetan mother and newborn for $65, literacy training for an Afghan girl for $75, safety of the Mayan rainforest for $100, and protection from female genital mutilation for $1000.

Her MISSIONmarket is located on the first floor of the Manhattan ABC Home store. Also available for purchase through her Web site, charitable contributions directed at 15 organizations can be arranged as gifts. Each gift brings attention to the work of each organization, ranging from the African Rainforest Conservancy to Women for Afghan Women. Each gift-giving opportunity is intended to lend a hand to make a better world by aligning purchases with personal values.

CARING ABOUT SERVICE

Few of us truly understand the spirit of service the way Paulette Cole does. She believes that each and every person needs to take on a social cause and commit to change—making a situation better, increasing awareness, or improving a financial picture.

Listen to Paulette's description of her own values development, and you will begin to understand her uncommon strengths and qualities.

"I feel like I came into this world with a certain set of values that developed and matured over time," she says. "I was always profoundly connected to spirit as a young child. I was the youngest of three children. My parents were very busy, so I had a lot of time alone. I think that that nurtured my connection to spirit. I had a deep connection with compassionate and loving people. I really felt people growing up. So, you know, I grew into caring about the injustices of humankind as I matured and developed. That set the tone for being more values-based in my work because that was in my heart. As you get older, life experience happens, and I've had a lot of challenges, and I've had a lot of loss [two of her three children died at three months of age], and those things strengthened my level of purpose. There was a level of choice for me: if I was going to do the work, and do it at this level, I needed to feel like I was productively in service. Otherwise I wouldn't put that type of demand on myself."

CO-CREATING VALUES AT WORK

Paulette believes that transparency and vulnerability are necessary to create a cultural shift in an organization. It is a very difficult thing to do. As a leader, her strengths are visual and creative. She has "ambassadors" with different skill sets who help guide people. "When I first came back to the company, we held a three-day senior team conference and we co-created our values. It was really amazing because part of me felt very intuitively that I was really the only one attached to these values. But I put them out there, and even though there were people who were here from before we made this shift, they agreed on the values that I had in my heart. It is really about human nature. As one of my friends says, there is the divine in everyone. Once given a chance to choose, I do believe they care about other people." The group "co-created" nine values. These included community, creativity, social responsibility, sustainability, service, spirit, integrity, passion, and acknowledgment.

"We are trying to be a model for other businesses and how they shift. Part of that is being willing to be scrutinized. Actively being in the action of shifting, actively trying to be transparent, we realize that there are those shadows. You have to be willing to go through that phase. And you have to realize that and be willing to deal. But this is a very difficult vision—it is our responsibility to keep people employed and to keep the economy growing. And sometimes that is in direct conflict with transparency and the values we have."

AFFECTING SOCIAL CHANGE AND REACHING OUT

Paulette's focus on societal change and injustice takes her away from one-on-one relationships. "I think there is something less intimate about the work I am doing now. I feel really driven at this point, but on a real macro-scale. I feel that the injustices are so extreme. Even though my work touches a lot of individuals, I think that to affect change, I must drive awareness. We need to step up to the plate and start to make changes to the constituencies that we have access to. Al Gore's movie on global warming, *An Inconvenient Truth,* is fundamentally about message, about how we are completely on the wrong track. We don't have the luxury to take it person by person. I think of Mother Theresa as a spiritual guide on some level, but at this point, I am not feeling like I can have the type of intimate relationships that she had. I want to try to affect things from a place that is larger than that. But what is really larger than that, though, when you ask the question. So there is some conflict in my mind."

Still, she was quick to point out these injustices: There are only two countries in the modern world that have not signed the Kyoto

Accord. American cars are *not* being built to the standards that others have around the world, like in China and Japan. These are injustices, and policy is not aiding the benefit of the greatest number of people. She also believes there is military injustice. So many people are starving around the world, and yet the military budget is still so large. "With just a little bit of that money so many of the people who are dying could be fed. We would still have the largest military budget in the world. But these people don't have a voice, they don't get that money, and that is an injustice."

REMEMBERING, LIKE THE QUEEN BEE

"My values are challenged everyday. I think that what I ultimately do is try to remember them." One of her mentors, Horst Rechelbacher from Aveda, gave her the metaphor of the queen bee. She initially denied it, until he explained that the queen bee's job was *to remember* where the flowers are. This metaphor helps her keep her values in the picture. "When I tap into my intuition, I believe it is something I need to do. And when I learn new things, I understand how it connects to the bigger picture. For me, this is an example of universal participation. There is something divine, some divine intervention. I am plugged into a purpose."

Cole believes that we each have one single purpose that no one else has. We have information inside of us that we have to put out there. "It is also about empowering our intentions and to really make a choice. I chose to come back here and I chose to get on this path. I chose to transition this business, but all I had was the intention—the intention to bring purpose and values into a business. You have to hold the intention, and *remember* it, just like in meditation when you come back to your breath.

"I was really depressed a couple of weeks ago. I was feeling like there is this tipping point being out there creating the ripples. I began to wonder 'Am I doing anything?' Am I really having an impact? And then I remembered being in a healing place, where the bottom line is that human feeling and caretaking." She recalls when her two boys,

16 years ago and eight years ago, died at three months of age of the same disease. Each time she went through it, she remembered that place of caretaking and healing. Just recently, when she cancelled all her meetings at work to show up for a claustrophobic friend's MRI, she recalled it again. "I had to stand completely contorted with my hand in the MRI for a half hour. When I was there, I felt something about being there that is more meaningful than anything." Her friend was fine, but it took her back to that place. "On a deep, deep level, I feel like that is my professional purpose. I feel so close to it. My purpose is to magnify the caretaking and the loving in business and leadership. That kind of feminine balance of intuition and creativity, that the maternal kind of energetic push can really be successful in a paternal paradigm. But I have to tell you on the day-to-day basis I don't necessarily feel like I can do that. I am working towards it, and remembering and forgetting it, and *remembering*."

10

Step 2—
Ask, "Who Am I?"

"The unexamined life is not worth living."
SOCRATES

*"As a child I was told and believed that there was a treasure buried beneath every rainbow.
I believed it so much that I have been unsuccessfully chasing rainbows most of my life. I wonder why no one ever told me that the rainbow and the treasure were both within me."*

**JOAN FOUNTAIN (posted outside a store
near Yale University in New Haven, Connecticut)**

Our second step is: Ask, "Who am I?" We must get to know our personal values, strengths, and needs. These are the glorious qualities that make us shine.

What do you do with this information? Knowing who you are and what your needs are can help to identify activities for personal growth. What do you want to achieve, learn, acquire, and master in the workplace? How can you find ways to achieve your personal goals? What can the work environment do to facilitate your personal growth? The workplace should value more than the bottom line. It must become a pathway to personal growth. Each individual characteristic and need can be matched with at least one activity or action. These become our individual growth goals and plans.

Quit hiding your treasures, if you do. Present them in the everyday life of your workplace. Find your creative voice deep inside. Give yourself space to breathe. Take time to explore and express. Develop all your skills, from the intuitive to the technical. Nurture your unique gifts. You are a source of light. You can be brilliant. You can illuminate your entire organization.

- - -

Valuing the Small Voice Inside

Kevin Melville Jennings
Healer and counselor

More than a decade ago, Kevin Melville Jennings left a successful job to embark on a new life's mission: to serve as an esoteric healer. In his words, "an esoteric healer is someone who works with concepts, myths, and symbols, and has an appreciation for patterns and energy flows. It is somebody who is able to look beyond science for healing solutions. The point is not to disregard science, but in a true metaphysical sense, to go beyond physics." His friends thought he had gone crazy. He was frightened, yet he believed in his journey.

There were moments when Jennings felt weak, when he was scared and uncertain of his choice. At his previous job he was comfortable; he knew what to expect. On his new path there was no guide to tell him what to do. However, it was something he felt he had to do. Now, looking back, Jennings feels that one choice has shaped his life, helped define him, and what he has to offer.

Now, his whole life is about helping others focus on their inner discovery to ask, "Who am I?" He describes his mission this way: "I think the only thing that really can save our planet is self-realization. It's not going to come from the outside. Nor is it going to come from the leaders, because it is not about being led; it's about making a kind of inner discovery."

LEARNING TO LIVE FROM THE HEART

Jennings is an ardent student of history who values the metaphysical. He believes that we should not be bound merely by what we see and feel; rather, we should use our knowledge to move beyond the restrictions of our current way of thinking—to look around to help us look within. Jennings's value system comes from this ideology.

"It is interesting that the word *value* comes from the same derivation as the word *valor*," he remarks. "To stay true to your values requires a kind of valor, which I call courage, which comes from the French word *coeur*—meaning the heart, heartfulness, and heartedness. So I basically look at my values as a constellation of love, stillness, and wisdom—and this philosophy is implemented by valuing courage, and striving to live from the heart."

To live these values is not easy. To remain loving in the face of hatred and competition requires commitment. To be still, calm, and insightful in a chaotic world takes discipline. To have wisdom amongst confusion and uncertainty takes strength.

"In my personal life, I try to keep myself aligned with courage, to push myself. Basically to come to live more from my heart and to try to get myself back on track when I realize that I'm not doing that."

FINDING THE ORDINARY EXTRAORDINARY

The measuring sticks in business are clear: profits, growth, revenues, and sales. These are external standards. We have convinced ourselves that success is reaching some arbitrary bar set by others, but we never realize that the bar is always going to be out of reach.

"I want people to understand that developing and cultivating the self is the key to happiness; that it doesn't exist outside," Jennings says. "I think part of the problem in the world today is that people are almost relentlessly externally focused. We are taught by and indoctrinated with images and bombarded by other people's philosophies. If the value of the self and the understanding that happiness and the pursuit of happiness is the same as the pursuit of self-realization, then people can take root in themselves. As they take root in the substance of their own being, they are able to discern, in a sense turn off the outside images, and open more within, so that a kind of balance or harmony is restored."

Money, titles, and pictures on the front pages of newspapers are simply symbols of what people perceive success must look like. However, external achievement is always empty and ephemeral because it lasts only as long as people are willing to pay attention. Instead, Jennings recognizes that joy comes from knowing ourselves. That type of happiness does not require riches.

"Something I have struggled within my own growth is to understand that the ordinary is where the extraordinary is found," he says. "Matter is not divorced from spirit; they are the same thing; and we don't have to look any farther than our bodies to contact the sacred. It is not out there someplace else; it is inside, and everyone is or embodies this sacred temple."

To Jennings, life is about striving to know that our bodies are sacred temples. By examining, understanding, and accepting whom we are, life opens itself up to new opportunities and relationships.

TURNING INWARD

Jennings recognizes the difficulty of his job; he understands the hesitancy of those he encounters. After all, much of our society is based on the idea that the reward for hard work is money and fame.

"My professional mission is to try to be a new paradigm of a new expression of love, embodying this relationship between the sacred and the physical," he says. "I would say my professional mission is to help others find and reach self-realization. It is to help them create a home or a place to be able to do that—to find themselves."

In today's fast-paced, competition-filled, media-saturated world, the seemingly simple ideal of self-realization seems hidden under a cloud of confusion. Future leaders must work to create environments where individuals feel comfortable turning inward.

INHERITING THE FAMILY VALUES

Jennings comes from a Celtic family, primarily Scottish and Irish, and his relatives maintain a love and respect for their heritage. As a child he was taught a set of values that have been passed down for generations.

"When my grandparents would come over or our extended family would get together, one of the things that we used to do when I was little was read poetry," he remembers. "And older members of the family often had their favorite poems, and they became like "the greatest hits" request. I didn't think much of it at the time, but as I have gotten older I think it's one of the most valuable gifts I was ever given as a child."

When Jennings was six years old, he got the measles. To raise his spirits his father bought him a present: a book on King Arthur and the knights of the roundtable. Jennings was mesmerized by the stories and the chivalry that the knights exhibited through their quest for the Holy Grail. The story planted the seeds of one of his core values—the idea of living from the heart.

"Among my family there was this teaching, a real participation between the adults and the children," he says. "There was a real appreciation of art, a profound respect for it, and there was the exchange, the experience of having it be something shared. I think those values are a lot of qualities that have influenced my whole life."

ELIMINATING THE SHAME

There is tremendous pressure on individuals to conform to external molds of what they ought to be and what they ought to achieve. Individuals who choose to go outside these predetermined norms are ridiculed. Jennings understands the danger of this restrictive view and how harmful it can be to push others down.

"I think one of the greatest agents of harm is shame," Jennings says. "Messages of shame are the messages that isolate and fragment people from their truth, from their integrity. And it's amazing how much shame is used in our culture to control people or to keep them from feeling empowered."

People will do almost anything to avoid shame. A focus on shame drives people apart, reminding them of what they are missing instead of what they have. It makes people think that they are somehow lacking.

"Leaders use shame as a means of controlling, because they use that to create dividedness—dividing the self from the self, dividing people against each other, fragmenting and isolating people," says Jennings.

AVOIDING THE LEAST COMMON DENOMINATOR

A leader must balance the desire to respect the individuals of his team, with the need to garner the greatest collective result. For Jennings, the individual is what the group is all about: "The individual is the microcosm of the group. The energy of the group comes from the individual."

To ignore the individual is to forget the unique talent everyone possesses. A leader that only looks at the collective whole is limited to noticing only the similarities between individuals. "If you put your focus on the group it often means that you are going to speak to the level of the least common denominator, whereas if you address the individual, you unlock the extraordinary and you begin to access the group's unique resources," Jennings says.

CONNECTING WITH THE HEART

Many business leaders think the cure for the recent plague of high employee turnover is simply to raise salaries. They feel that anyone can be lured by the promise of riches, bonuses, and stock options. Yet while that may get them in the door, Jennings understands that these trappings will not make people stay.

"People leave when they feel unconnected or that their life is meaningless in a sense, or that the company will just hire somebody else, or that their greater good is elsewhere, or they think 'Screw them—they never gave me my due anyway.' I think that the way to encourage commitment and loyalty is to be committed and loyal. It's about focusing on the person that goes deeper than what they do, that sees the job that the person does in relationship to the individual doing it," Jennings says.

Employees want a connection that goes beyond a paycheck. Individuals want to know that they matter and what they do matters. "Loyalty is in the heart," believes Jennings. "If someone connects to someone else through the heart, even if it is a business relationship, it doesn't matter; a connection has been made."

Reaching out to connect to another person has a profound impact. It nurtures a deeper relationship, acknowledges the strengths inside, and initiates a focus on "Who am I?"

PUTTING THE HUMAN ABOVE THE WORK

Work is what we do, but it need not define who we are. When leaders see employees only through the work they do, they devalue their humanity. Jennings recognizes that this creates an inherent distance between the leader and those around him.

"I think leaders form bonds with people by being a human being and through understanding that the human takes precedent over the worker," he says. "If a person feels connected to, seen, and valued above and beyond the work they do, or what they help to facilitate, then their life has purpose and meaning, and they are going to stay around."

Instead of forming bonds with others and raising individuals up, leaders today purposefully keep others at a distance below them. Jennings is saddened by the fact that people find comfort in power over others.

"Too many leaders see people as a resource for consumption," he says. "These leaders are entrenched in depersonalizing, in not connecting through the heart. Leaders in depersonalizing institutions are interested in acquiring or maintaining power at the expense of fostering open expression and passionate dialogue. Leaders like this are interested in power and oppose self-empowerment. They think that if others gain power, then they lose power; they don't understand the idea of collective empowerment."

FACING DEATH AND SEEING THE TRUTH WITHIN

Years ago, Jennings survived a battle with testicular cancer. The ordeal was frightening and forced him to consider the meaning of his life. It helped reshape his values and his thinking, and he emerged even more confident in his beliefs.

"I think up until that point I had lived my life from the perspective of what I should be doing rather than what I want to be doing," he says. "When I had to face mortality, I realized that I needed to live from my heart. Really knowing that I am only going to be here a certain amount of time galvanized me to wake up, to make it count, because I could have in a lot of ways been like Rip Van Winkle, and just let life go drifting by. I needed the courage to begin really living life from my heart."

People are all too eager to tell you what they think is right and wrong, and each one is more confident that they speak the truth. Jennings realized that in the end the only standards that matter are your own.

"It was easier and less challenging to live by other people's rules, and my former beliefs of what I thought was right or wrong, or what a successful life was," he says. "What I was forced to confront was that if I had died at that time, I realized that I would have spent my entire life striving to get somewhere that I never really wanted to reach. So I vowed that if I were going to live, I was going to live each day as if I had already arrived, which for me meant living from the heart."

Courageously, Kevin Jennings does indeed live from his heart, as he encourages others to turn inward and find the ordinary extraordinary.

CLEAN THE SLATE

To clean the slate means to let go of our past mishaps, hardships, and negative experiences. Hanging on to past grievances, unfair practices, and hurtful relationships does no good.

Admit your mistakes and the mistakes of others. Forgive yourself and others who have intentionally, or, more often than not, unintentionally harmed you. Start fresh. Work through some of the past "baggage" or "unfinished business." An open and accepting mind-set will better enable you to embrace your new leadership construct and definition of success.

DISCOVERING THE SELF

There are four ways to explore and discover "Who am I?": getting in touch with your personal values; getting in touch with your personal characteristics and needs; taking a close look at your strengths and weaknesses; and exploring the factors that have shaped your values.

Get in Touch with Your Personal Values

A value is something that is important to you. It defines who you are, what you believe in, and what you cherish. Values influence the choices we make, the way we invest our energy and time, the people we choose to be close to, and the interests we pursue. In difficult times, they serve as a compass amid conflicting demands and varying points of view. To lay a foundation for a life that is meaningful and satisfying, you must know exactly what your personal values are.

Here's what we want you to do: Take out a sheet of paper and write down your personal values. Although this identification process sounds simple, it requires some serious thought and reflection. A few guidelines are helpful: Recognize the intrinsic worth, strengths, and merit of your values. Share them. Acknowledge and support the values cited by others; and encourage open discussions on the topic of values.

Understanding your values creates greater harmony in a group. There is an awareness of what's important to each group member. Leaders can use this information to help plan what to do with work time, free time, weekends, and vacations in order to tap into an individual's interests.

Get in Touch with Your Personal Characteristics and Needs

Take a piece of paper and note the characteristics that best answer these two questions "Who am I?" and "What are my needs?" Do some in-depth thinking. Write down at least three qualities that best describe your individual traits and needs.

- Who am I?
- What are my needs?

Take a Close Look at Your Strengths and Weaknesses

Be up close and personal, and look at your strengths and weaknesses. It is important to recognize the things you do well (your strengths) and don't do well (your weaknesses) so you can recognize how they reflect the needs of a group. To get started, use this checklist of questions. Think about each one deeply and definitively.

1. Do I communicate openly by expressing my own feelings and emotions?
2. Do I take risks?
3. Do I suggest ideas that I believe might promote the achievement of the group's goals?
4. Do I actively listen?
5. Am I sensitive and empathetic to individual needs?
6. Do I help others experience success?

7. Do I frequently use descriptive praise?
8. Do I ask for feedback on how well I am communicating and interacting with each group member?
9. Do I stimulate self-initiated growth and personalized learning?
10. Do I give sufficient freedom to learn?
11. Do I frequently use humor?
12. Do I ask group members how I could improve?
13. Do I stimulate creative and intuitive thinking?

Then, complete the following strengths and weaknesses exercise by filling in the answers on a piece of paper.

1. What are my five greatest strengths and weaknesses?

   Strengths:
   1.
   2.
   3.
   4.
   5.

   Weaknesses:
   1.
   2.
   3.
   4.
   5.

2. "I disappoint members of the group, when I . . . ."

3. "I can really motivate a group member, when I . . . ."

Explore the Factors That Have Shaped Your Values

Think about your own values. What are their origins? How have they changed? Four factors usually shape our values:

1. Family and childhood experiences
2. Personal relationships with significant individuals
3. Major life changes and learning experiences
4. Conflict events that produce self-discovery

Combined with our own learning, these factors transform our values over time. Let's take a close look at each.

Family and childhood experiences. During childhood, parents, family members, siblings, peers, teachers, and religious organizations share their beliefs and shape our values. Our childhood experiences from school, family rituals, holidays and celebrations, travel and vacations, as well as daily family life all work together to form our core values.

Personal relationships with significant individuals. There are a handful of individuals that we meet in our daily lives who really "connect" with us. Teachers, classmates, bosses, co-workers, or friends can all be special role models whom we look up to, respect, admire, and want to emulate. Their values greatly influence the formation of our own.

Major life changes and learning experiences. Marriage, rearing children, taking a new job or position, moving to a new location, confronting the death of a significant other, or adjusting to the departure of children from home all cause our values to shift and evolve over time. Discovering new motivations, emotions, and conflicts within ourselves can bring new light to old beliefs that we have always taken for granted. Learning more about ourselves, others, and how to deal with different people invites us to examine and reinvent our values. For example, an adolescent's first romance can often open up huge new avenues to self-discovery.

Conflict events that produce self-discovery. Wars, environmental disasters, community crime, government programs, legal reforms, and other sources of externally-driven conflict often transform our values in deep and lasting ways.

Life is full of forces that cause us to examine and re-examine our values. Discovering how our values are shaped provides greater insight into who we are and what we might become. While each of the four factors can transform our values, they are not owned until they are examined through introspection.

11

Step 3—
Ask, "Who Are You?"

"Look at your eyes.
They are so small but they see enormous things."
RUMI

"My feeling is that the individual is what counts," says Jerry Fisher, retired VP of Corporate R & D at Baxter Healthcare. "You must understand the individual to have a basis for a strong infrastructure, and if you don't value and nurture the individual, then you have no chance with the team. An Irish saying that caught my attention was: 'You know those rock fences that go everywhere in Ireland—made of big rocks and little rocks? You know what the little rocks are for? They hold up the big rocks.'" We certainly agree. The "little rocks" play a critical role. Focus must be placed in all organizations on learning about others and their individual needs.

Our third step is: Ask, "Who are you?" We too often forget to really *see* the persons next to us. Unquestionably, they too have an abundance of gifts, ready to be shared. This chapter is about learning how to look into the eyes of others and to get to know who they really are. While they may be small, they, in the words of Rumi, "see enormous things."

While individuals in a group must give attention to their own needs and interests, they must also interact with other group members and help them address their needs and interests. All work settings must encourage their members to have this double focus. Learn what makes your fellow workers unique and brilliant by knowing their strengths and resources. Each person can shine individually, but taken together; the light from all will make your organization glow.

Connecting Passionately with People

Kaethe Morris Hoffer
Private feminist lawyer and activist

When Kaethe Morris Hoffer connects with people, the earth shakes. More often than not, there are titanic reverberations. Hoffer is a private feminist lawyer and activist, focused on equality and justice in a world in which power is abused. Time and time again, she makes a difference not only in gender-related issues like domestic violence, sexual assault, and reproductive health care, but also in the areas of poverty, discrimination, and HIV/AIDS.

Hoffer and her husband, Matt, are a straight couple who are passionate about gay rights. Even though they were married at a Quaker gathering in her hometown in 1999, they did not apply for an actual marriage license. They refused to support a law that treats gay and straight people differently, what they call "discriminatory application of the laws." In 2004, when the Massachusetts Supreme Judicial Court ruled that same-sex couples have a constitutional right to marry, the couple flew to Boston to finally legalize their marriage.

Without a marriage license, however, they endured many of the same financial hardships common to lesbian and gay couples. They filed taxes separately; they realized that neither would receive their spousal Social Security or Medicare benefits in old age; they paid $500 to legally change their names, a fee that is waived for newlyweds; and budgeted as much as $5,000 a year for her health insurance when she left her job to have a baby, because their marriage was not recognized by the state. Now that they are officially married, they plan to donate that $5,000 to "Freedom to Marry," the New York-based advocacy organization leading the gay-marriage charge.

••

Hoffer makes a difference by simply getting to know the needs of people and groups. In 1997, she worked as a civil attorney for the Legal Assistance Foundation of Chicago, which provides civil legal representation to impoverished Chicago residents. She served on the Governor's Commission on the Status of Women in Illinois from 1999 to 2003, where she chaired the commission's Violence Reduction Working Group. She is the co-author of the Illinois Gender Violence Act. This law says that sexual violation is unlawful sexual discrimination; victims can sue their rapist in civil court whether or not the criminal justice system ever charged or prosecuted the assault.

Hoffer is devoted to representing survivors of sexual assault and domestic violence. She believes it will take civil lawsuits to prove that rapists can be taken to task for their sexual violation. She believes that taking a stand, refusing to tolerate sexual violation, and working together to eradicate it are absolutely necessary to address this astonishing and frightening fact: according to the United States Department of Justice, one in every ten American women are raped.

THE POWER OF KINDNESS

"In many ways," Hoffer asserts, "kindness has become more and more central to my values. I think that the power of connecting with people in a loving way regardless of the circumstances has proven to me to be the most unexpected agent for positive change. My mother is really a remarkable woman when it comes to understanding. Her emotional intelligence is just phenomenal and I have learned a huge amount from her."

Such a simple gift: to let a person know that you see who they are. Hoffer is an expert at it. We can all learn from her steadfast style and sensitive spirit. She has this to offer: "I am very attentive to the skills or things that my co-workers value in themselves and are proud of. I am able, pretty readily, to know what it is about a person that I can pay attention to, what it is that people do to resonate their best selves. And by attending to that, I think it is actually very simple to send people messages that value that—whether by inquiring about a particular thing, or by always appreciating whatever it is that they have done in whatever way they contribute.

"Also, I think that people try to do their best and want to be more productive. They want to be central and more needed, valued, appreciated, and seen. I treat everybody the same way, and part of that means being aligned to what it is that they value and what things make them light up. I do the same in every work environment that I have been in."

Hoffer learned how to do this when she was a junior in high school. She discovered that the way to be happy was to avoid the cliquish group dynamics, where kids treated each other badly, because there was a massive lack of appreciation and understanding. She simply interacted with people one on one and found out what his or her "special thing" was. This involved, in her words, "interacting with them in a way that would uncover their passions so that I could talk with them about something meaningful to them. I was able to have these wonderful interactions with people as individuals." If the act of charitable behavior to other people defines kindness, then Hoffer is a kindness professional.

At the heart of her actions is respect. "When I was in junior high, I remember saying something to my mom about how much I hated gossip," she recalls. "My mom said gossip has a function, and it is very important to convey respect, and not be above it. Gossip plays a really serious role in communication, and that by sort of going, 'ugh, I don't do that,' you really alienate yourself as being able to participate. And you can participate in a loving way by acting like you are accepting normal gossip, but you are actually sharing positive public things. So, you model the kinds of things that people talk about and the kinds of stories that you tell, so that you are always open to the talk around the water cooler, you know. You participate in it, but you choose the ways in which you participate. And it is powerful in that sense."

INTERVENING TO OFFER SUPPORT

Hoffer says, "Then, when there are really important things that need to be dealt with, when you can't model the change, I look for opportunities to face the conflict. For example, with the problems between my supervisor and my co-worker, I spent a lot of time talking with my co-worker, who was open about the particular problem, and making sure that she felt supported. Then I explained to her that I was really concerned about this, and that one of the things I was considering doing was going and talking to her boss. Not on her behalf, but in part because my concern was that the situation was getting so bad that I was going to lose her or the organization was going to lose her. She was very valuable to our organization. I ended up initiating a series of conversations with my boss about the problem, and giving advice about her disconnection.

"My interventions are done in a kind, caring, and smart manner. I think people are able to feel my support. I think that I am able to convey the message that says essentially 'I am sharing this with you; I think you can do better; I think the situation could be better.' I wouldn't do an intervention if I did not believe there could be a better outcome, and believing that there could be a better outcome means believing that whomever it is that I do an intervention with has the potential to do better personally."

To Hoffer, success is earning enough trust for someone to be vulnerable with her.

"If someone comes to me and is comfortable telling me that they were unhappy or something like that, then that is a success that I have created," she says. "I aspire to feel like a confidant to a huge number of people within all levels of the agency." Her ability to know "Who are you?" and "What are your needs?" is rare indeed.

Finding Success in Touching Others

Jack Riopelle
Former chairman of
Wisconsin Film & Bag

One of the most difficult things for a leader to do is to define success. Effective leaders are rarely satisfied with the status quo. For many CEOs, this means a constant push for greater profits. For Jack Riopelle, the chairman of Wisconsin Film & Bag, success is not quite as tangible, yet far more meaningful.

Riopelle says, "My biggest measurement for success is whether or not I have accomplished what I believe to be my mission in business and personal life, and that is 'Did I really make others' lives better?' And not just monetarily—did I make them feel better about themselves? Did I make them feel like they were capable of achieving more than they ever thought they could? And if there are a number of people who attribute that to me, then I would have to say that I am successful."

INVESTING IN HUMAN DEVELOPMENT

Finite financial and capital resources force organizations to make difficult choices in their investments. Businesses are always looking at ways to cut costs, increase productivity, and improve efficiency. However, organizations would often be better served developing an incredibly valuable resource they already possess, a resource that is consistently under-utilized: their employees.

"The organizations that have a better chance of staying together are the organizations that have an ongoing practice of human development taking place, so that individuals recognize that even if they stay in the same position, they have a chance to grow inside that position," Riopelle says. "And part of that is inspiring, nurturing, and cultivating individual strengths and talents. You need development to do that. It's one thing for a leader to verbalize that but it's another to put words into actions by creating an atmosphere where development is real."

Riopelle understands that empowering employees can have tangible benefits. When leaders motivate those around them, it pays dividends in terms of increased productivity and efficiency. Workers need to know that they are valued; people want to hear that they are capable of greatness.

"I hope that I inspire people by convincing them that they are capable of far more than they thought they were," Riopelle says. "As I say to my employees, as often as I can, 'it's not where you're from that counts, it's who you are inside as a person that counts.' And just because you're from a small town, just because you're from a poor family, just because you're from a dysfunctional family, just because you didn't go to the right school, whatever the perceived barrier is, it doesn't matter where you're from. It matters who you are. And if you focus on who you are and not where you're from, you have a better chance of getting individuals to see that they can compete, that they can grow, that they can take on more than they ever thought they could. And I think that's what a leader needs to do."

LEARNING FROM FAILURE

It seems odd that a leader would be excited by failure, but Riopelle is. He recognizes that failure is a natural part of life; if we are not failing occasionally then we must not be trying hard enough. Riopelle views failure as an opportunity to grow personally and professionally. In the wake of missed expectations, one can become dejected and look outward, or one can look inside and determine what to take from the experience and move forward as a stronger leader.

"We learn more from failure, and how we rebound from failure, than we do from success, and I think it is probably the most important mark of what your character is and who you are as a person," he says. "You can become finicky; you can become filled with hate and envy for others who are successful. Or you can say, 'what did I learn and how do I take what I learned and make sure I avoid this from happening again?' You can use failure as a source of strength and learn from it. So clearly failures in my life have been the things that I have learned the most from."

CREATING CONNECTIONS WITH EMPLOYEES

Leaders must ask themselves: "Whom are you trying to impress?" The people who work under you likely do not care about the size of your bonus, your stock options, or your access to the corporate jet. Riopelle and others we interviewed understand that leaders gain strength by creating connections with, not distance from, employees. There are four ways to create connections with others: knowing the needs and characteristics of group members, helping them experience success, using descriptive praise to motivate and facilitate personal growth, and giving advice on how to improve.

Know the Needs and Characteristics of Others in the Group

As group members, we must learn to do things for other group members. Focus on the others within your group. Pick a professional partner or colleague. Look at her and think about what makes her unique. What are her strengths and needs? Do some in-depth thinking. Now take a piece of paper and note the characteristics that best answer these two questions about her:

- Who are you?
- What are your needs?

Now list three or more characteristics after each question that best describe a particular co-worker. It is important to recognize the things she or he does well. When you have completed your descriptions, share this information to begin getting to know them. How accurate was your description compared to his or her self-description? In some cases, they may be very close. In others, they may be quite different. As the group goes forward, members will become more aware of each other's needs and characteristics. Then, there will be clarity as to what each person brings to the group. A team can be built that reflects the needs of the entire group.

Help Others Experience Personal Success

When people feel good about themselves because of success in their workplace, this positive feeling will have a spillover effect. These individuals will perform better, seek more responsibility, and accomplish more in their work. Because of continued successes, they are more apt to take risks. They will try to do things that are more difficult for them because they have experienced earlier success—and risk-taking enables learning and discovery.

By identifying employees' greatest strengths and matching them with responsibilities and tasks that draw upon their strengths, leaders will increase the chances of employee success. It's important to "rig" small successes to some extent. It does no good to put employees into situations, roles, groups, or activities where there is a good chance of failure. Continuous failure breeds only one thing—more failure. It becomes a self-fulfilling prophecy. Self-confidence is weakened, and it is more and more difficult for the individual to achieve success.

Managing and "staging" a few small wins for employees increases inner value and self-worth. This, in turn, improves their self-esteem and fortifies their own skill base. This begins to feed positively on itself and brings more success. Individuals expect success and perpetuate it themselves.

Use Descriptive Praise to Motivate and Facilitate Personal Growth

We can facilitate the development of others by using descriptive praise. This is a technique that is very useful with children, too. In their classic book *Liberated Parents Liberated Children,* Adele Faber and Elaine Mazlish find that words that evaluate tend to hinder a child; words that describe set the child free. If a child has done something well, rather than say, "you did a great job," it is much better to describe what you saw and felt when the child did it. Describing the child's work in detail adds a whole new dimension to the child's view of himself or herself and creates a motivated learner.

For example, if a child built a birdhouse and showed it to her mother, one response might be, "Good work!" This is merely global praise. It is not a bad response, but specific, descriptive praise would be much better because the child would learn more about herself. Accordingly, the mother could respond by saying something like, "How warm the birds will be when they live in it; the color you painted it will help to camouflage the birds; it reminds me of one I saw in the pet store recently that housed bluebirds." Now, the child looks at herself differently. The child has built a shelter to house birds from the elements and intruders, and because bluebirds live in similarly built structures, they could possibly inhabit this birdhouse. This child is more motivated to learn than the one who was simply congratulated.

Telling an employee that she has done a "good job" is not good enough. This response *limits* learning and growth. It would be better to point out a number of things that never would have occurred to the employee. For example, if she gave a presentation, she could be told that she helped to teach some especially important information using a very effective style of presenting material; or that it was done in such a way as to make the audience enjoy itself; or that her style left everyone feeling very unified and hopeful for improvement. This descriptive praise adds a whole new dimension to the employee's view of herself. Now the workplace has a motivated employee.

Give Advice on How to Improve

Leaders also need to be able to provide those employees who warrant constructive criticism with proactive advice on how to improve. This advice should also be descriptive. It must specifically describe what an employee can do to shore-up a development need or correct a weakness. Leaders can translate constructive feedback into an action plan for the employee. For example, if an employee has been told he is not a good writer or presenter, then the leaders might recommend a specific public speaking class. If an employee's marketing plans are not creative, then the leader can suggest ways to weave more innovative thinking into her future planning activities. If an accountant is told that her projections don't include the needs of a particular department, then the leader can suggest ways to work with this group to build their needs and estimates into the overall budget picture. Rather than saying, "This person has a problem" it is better to say, "This person requires a different response." The leader focuses *not* on the faults of employees, but on what needs to be done to improve their performance.

Just like parents, leaders can help build and strengthen self-image using behavior and experiences. The parent knows the child's past achievements and can share this information to provide encouragement and comfort. Similarly, the leaders of the workplace should also have a well-stocked warehouse of information, past achievements where the employee has done something particularly well. Drawing on past information to fortify the employee's self-esteem is an important role of the leader.

Ultimately, if employees have heard over and over again that they have special abilities and positive qualities then the leader is helping them to believe in their own strengths and understand who they are. Effective leaders should be actively involved in giving this positive reinforcement to all employees. This provides workers with self-knowledge and recognition by telling them again and again what their special qualities are using illustrative words as descriptive-action steps.

12

Step 4— Find Common Ground

"The noblest pleasure is the joy of understanding."
LEONARDO DA VINCI

"Take into account that great love and great achievements involve great risk."
THE DALAI LAMA

Brian Sorge says, "I think foresight is very important. A lot of times people are living in the moment and don't understand that what they are doing has a long-term impact. All actions have consequences and they are probably more extensive than you can ever imagine."

Sorge's job is to know people and to know their strengths and weaknesses. He knows what motivates them and what irritates them. More than anything else, he has the ability to bring people together. He is an expert at our fourth step: finding common ground.

Sorge has made his living helping organizations assemble diverse and effective teams. As the former director of North American recruiting for Marakon Consulting, he was responsible for identifying the best and the brightest of the business world. Currently, he serves as an executive at Lambert & Associates, a consulting firm where he helps companies build more diverse and inclusive corporate environments. To build an inclusive team, however, it is first necessary for its members to be able to find their own common ground.

Step four focuses on finding the common links between people. It means discovering their overlapping interests and intentions as well as creating new goals and objectives that all team members share. Finding common ground must be done diligently and consistently. It is very easy to take the path of least resistance—that is, to simply mandate what needs to be done. It is a far different thing to create a path that leverages everyone's strengths, makes everyone a part of the solution, and enables them to function as a well-oiled group.

When employees spend time finding common ground, they are far more able and willing to see leaders as facilitators, peers, and equals at work. They know how to listen deeply and care profoundly. Group members not only help each other answer "Who am I?" and "What are my needs?" but also focus on "Who are we?" and "What are our needs?" Rather than just following a leader, the people now lead themselves.

When a group establishes common bonds, the result can be a collection of an extraordinary pool of skills, knowledge, expertise, and experience. Most leaders do not take advantage of this power source. Have you sought an answer to a difficult question that has been troubling you from your co-workers? What comes back can be phenomenal! This collective thinking surfaces ideas of all kinds. Brainstorming together is a powerful tool. When a group of caring individuals gets involved, the idea of one member serves as a catalyst for another.

Using the collective knowledge of the group is a formidable skill that more leaders should engage in. Instead, they sometimes hide out in their office. They are afraid to admit that they don't know the answer to a question. Doesn't this make them appear weak and unknowledgeable to their employees? Aren't leaders supposed to have all the solutions? No, they're not. If leaders will open their doors, express their vulnerabilities, and say to their group, "Let's solve this difficult problem together," they will receive better results from everyone.

RISK-AVERSION PREVENTS "COMING TOGETHER"

Big organizations are not very good at failure. They cannot accept or recognize it or adopt the perspective required for people to take risks. In baseball, however, the guys who hit the most home runs are the ones who always swing the bat even though they frequently strike out.

Risk-aversion seems to be the watchword of many companies. While risk-aversion may grow the bottom line in the short-term, taking risks and encouraging innovation is what accelerates growth and stimulates creativity for the long-term. Sadly, most companies still do not understand that risk-averse managers and employees do not feel comfortable creating new products, services, or categories. They end up creating line extensions, improvements, and upgrades, and close-in enhancements. Financial windfalls never materialize; the risk profile is just too low.

When risk-aversion takes root, it impacts the culture. Isolation and anomie creep in. People do not open up, convey their opinions, or feel comfortable making bold statements. They hide. They are afraid of losing their jobs. No one is sure from one day to the next what may happen. Employees will never discover common ground in this type of environment. They may not even get through step one of our change process to ask, "Who am I?" They will not want others to know who they are.

Dean Kamen, inventor of the Segway People Mover, strongly believes in creating a culture where people accept failure as an intrinsic part of successful innovation. He believes in cultivating a risk-taking mindset: "We weren't competing with anybody else," he says of a new product. "We were competing with a technical challenge that, if we solved it, people would have access to something that would make their lives better, and we'd make a lot of money to boot."

Encouraging employees to think innovatively and explore new business ideas helps to achieve new levels of success. When risk-taking is nurtured, a more open, informal, and creative mind-set emerges which, in turn, enables people to more easily find common ground with each other.

Identifying and Tackling Consumer Problems

Dean Kamen
President of DEKA Research

Dean Kamen makes a living finding problems—that is, consumer problems that he can solve with new products and new technologies. He has no interest in searching for ways to improve existing products and services. The holder of more than 150 patents in sectors ranging from healthcare to transportation to the environment, Kamen does not take the road less traveled—he builds a brand new highway.

There is no denying that his Segway vehicle is an engineering marvel. Developed at a cost of more than $100 million, Kamen's people-mover is an intricate bundle of hardware and software that mimics the human body's capacity to maintain its balance. It has no engine, no brakes, no gearshift, no throttle, and no steering wheel. The average rider can travel for an entire day using only five cents of electricity.

While Kamen's life purpose is to continue to make the world a better place, he also wants to make a lot of money. These goals are not incongruent. Why? Because bigger problems mean bigger solutions, which, in turn, create greater value. So his reason for making more money isn't just to inflate his bank account; it's to enable more and greater innovation. He keeps raising the bar to find need-intensive problems and opportunities, and in the process, he finds common ground in grappling with the questions his team confronts—everything from the safety of the product to its pricing. The nature of finding this type of common ground extends from employees inside to consumers and customers outside. It is actually a huge insight when companies recognize the need to go outside of their corporate walls and find the connection between their customer's needs and the company's internal strengths. The overlapping point can represent a core capability and future growth opportunity.

MERGING THE INDIVIDUAL AND TEAM INTO ONE

One of the hardest balances to strike is between encouraging freedom of the individual and harnessing the resources of a team to achieve specific goals. In the past, we have used the term "disciplined freedom" to describe this balance. However, leaders need to understand that the two are not mutually exclusive. Creating teams does not mean the death of the individual.

"In my organizations," says Dean Kamen, "I think our strength is that we do not differentiate between individuals and teams. You take this individual and he is awesome, and that individual and she is awesome. Each is a great contributor; you put them all together on this project because it needs multidisciplinary skills. And it turns out to be a great team, but is it a great team because there were ten great individual contributors? Or is each of them a great contributor because they were part of a great team?"

The benefits of teams are that they increase the scale and quality of what organizations can accomplish. The challenge of a leader is to create an organizational structure that galvanizes resources without constraining the creative freedom of employees.

"We expect an entire team to act as if they were one empowered individual," Kamen says. "Knowing that the whole team can succeed together or fail together is okay. I would rather have the whole team succeed or the whole team fail on one particular project than have average or mediocre performance on ten projects. The result is far bigger than any individual win or loss. These groups give us the best of all worlds with the extra size, capability, resources, and horsepower of a team without taking on the bureaucracy or oneness that creates predictability. We need to have some structures and teams that get large, but we like to maintain the spirit of individuality. Our teams are just mega-hyper individuals all working and communicating and cooperating collectively."

Kamen continues: "I would say the biggest measurable difference between our teams and the teams I see elsewhere is that other companies ensure each team is managed. We have a leader who manages budgets and schedules, but the team leader does *not* manage the people on the team. We don't have anybody managing anybody else. Our teams depend on cooperation and not management, communication and not bureaucracy. No team has any more rules associated with managing it than any individual does."

Dean's team members manage themselves. Wow! When employees begin to lead themselves and their teams, you know that employees become more effective at communication and interaction. What will disappear is the leader's mandate to the group on what needs to be done. It will be replaced by self-recognition of the tasks at hand and self-regulation of their execution.

FAILING IS OKAY

As the head of a research and development organization, Kamen must accept that not every product his company produces will be a success. The challenge lies in sustaining superior results in the face of inevitable failure.

"In our business, we find really important problems that represent an exciting challenge to solve, albeit they may be very difficult to address," he reveals. "However, I will say as long as there is a plausible shot that we may succeed, as long as we are prepared to fail at the task and not see it as failing as individuals, then we will accept the challenge. People get stronger from failures; they learn from their mistakes. We just keep checking that we are moving in the right direction, in which case we keep going, or we try something else until we either succeed or can say with confidence that we can't solve this problem. As long as everybody is honest with themselves about our successes and honest with ourselves about why and how we failed, we'll have an organization that over time can count on guaranteed success."

It is the willingness to honestly assess work that allows an organization to continue to grow in the face of adversity. Accepting failure as part of the business of innovation encourages people to take risks, fosters openness, and results in meaningful links between employees.

Kamen's company often finds itself with no one else to measure itself against. That innovative environment requires even greater internal motivation. With no competitive benchmark, employees must trust in the mission of the organization.

Kamen says, "People ask me, 'If there is one invention you could work on, what would it be? Would it be a device to help the disabled get around? Would it be a way to deliver chemotherapy?' I like to think all the projects we work on, if we succeed at them, will share in the fact that we did them in ways that other people wouldn't have thought of. People usually think of success as competing with other people and winning. If I knew somebody else could make a product that solves one of those problems, then I wouldn't bother. There are too many unsolved problems to work on."

DEALING WITH CHALLENGED VALUES

Values help to create a bond between people. Common values serve as a connecting point, something to which two persons can almost immediately relate. However, to get there, people have to be willing to share their personal values.

Sometimes values are challenged—and that is okay. It's how we deal with that challenge that opens us up to others and creates a connection. Kamen says, "In business, my values are challenged every day, all the time. We work on difficult projects and they rarely go according to schedule and budget; we have lots of pressures and demands, competing issues, competing clients. We build stuff that, if it doesn't work right, people die. I tell my people the same thing all the time, 'You figure out what's the right thing to do, not just what will appear right.' You sit with people and say, 'In a perfect world, what is the right thing to do.' Generally, if you say it that way and you mean it that way, it becomes much clearer."

Business decisions are not easy. It is healthy for leaders to question themselves and search within for an answer. Yet, too often individuals make things more complicated than they need to be; too often people rationalize a situation or bend a point of view.

"We live in a politically correct society where everybody is entitled to their opinion," Kamen says. "Well you know what? Everybody is not entitled to an opinion and there are things that are just wrong—period. There are things in this world that are right, and there are things that are wrong, and sure there is some gray in the middle, but when you look at most issues you need to say, 'What is the right thing? If there were no other issues, what would be the right thing to do?' When this is your approach, it never distracts you from what's right. Too often we allow ourselves to hide behind all the shades of gray that we've come to accept."

In short, creating an environment where people are vocal, willing to stand up for what they think is right, and challenge other opinions and viewpoints fosters understanding between people and ultimately common ground. The key to this, of course, is keeping a positive, buoyant, and nondefensive mind-set.

VALUING VERSUS JUST MANAGING PEOPLE

Employees are valuable assets; they are not commodities. They add incredible value to an organization.

"In today's time-crazed business world," comments Kamen, "everything is viewed as short-term and fungible. People buy and sell whole businesses and individuals become a part of those transactions. They hire 50 people, lay off 30 people, move the company, or sell the company. I don't think people are fungible. My business has products that can succeed and fail, that can be bought or sold, but people shouldn't be in the position to be bought and sold. People you nurture, people are a resource, and the company is an idea."

If an organization is spending significant resources monitoring and policing its employees, then the question must be asked, did they hire the right people? Companies gain value by motivating and encouraging workers, companies lose value with bloated management.

"People ask how can I manage my business and I tell them I don't," Kamen continues. "I have never hired a person that needs to be managed. If a person somehow slipped through, which is pretty rare considering how we hire people, that individual feels intimidated, like a fish out of water. Everyone sits around passionate about what they are doing and this person is thinking, 'I just wanted a job, I want to go home and do something else.' Well, they move on quickly because they don't fit. The culture is its own best Darwinian system of protecting what we value because if somebody is here without those values they are uncomfortable. As long as you have that, you don't need to spend any of your resources managing people."

When they truly value people, managers will be better able to understand employees' hot buttons and their cold buttons, what turns them off and what motivates them. This will enable managers and employees to find common ground.

• •

Bringing People Together

Brian Sorge
Vice President of
Client Solutions,
Lambert & Associates

Brian Sorge spent one year of high school on an exchange program in Venezuela. He lived with a host family with 12 children, and he quickly immersed himself into the foreign culture. Each day he would return to the unlocked house along with the other children and join in the family meals.

Thousands of miles away from home, weeks would go by without mail or any contact with his family. While Sorge's parents struggled with the separation, he relished the chance to gain a new perspective.

"When I went to Venezuela I got an objective sense of America," Sorge says. "I was there during the Reagan era when he was shot. I was there when the Pope was shot. I remember the whole issue was 'We don't like you because you are American.' They labeled me as different and that defined their attitudes towards me."

In Venezuela, Sorge was an outsider, and was judged based on all the stereotypes that the label carries. However, as he made the effort to meet people and they opened themselves up to him, they began to view him as a unique individual. It is always easier to define people by their differences and draw boundaries, but it is more valuable to look beyond.

"One of the most valuable learning exercises I have participated in at work involved compiling interviews of people on what it is like to be an outsider," Sorge says. "We probably did thousands of hours of interviews and the stories were amazing. It taught me that everyone is an outsider at some point in their lives and that by bringing him or her in you can have a real impact."

When you keep others outside, you will never benefit from their knowledge and talent. Only by bringing people in can you truly grow.

• •

JOINING A COMMUNITY

Being part of a community—whether it is a team, an organization, or a neighborhood—means being a part of something larger than yourself. There is a danger of getting lost in the crowd, of feeling insignificant and powerless. However, it is the interdependency of individuals that defines a strong community. Sorge realized very early the impact one person can make as a member of an effective community.

He says, "In Venezuela, I learned the value of commitment to the family, the sense that you can make a real contribution. We would go on these hikes up into the mountains to help some of the indigenous people. So from this little town in Ohio I had this amazing exposure to these things that just kind of fed into the value system that my parents and my family had instilled. Being part of a community you do whatever you can to contribute to and provide for other people."

A strong community is not homogenous. It is not created by finding individuals with similar backgrounds and experiences. A powerful community is defined by a common sense of purpose that provides the platform upon which diverse and different individuals can come together, share insights, and form a high-powered team.

"I love creating groups. I find ways to bring people together from all walks of life, to find commonalities and become friends," Sorge says. "They make connections and build a sense of community. I am able to create conversations devoid of nastiness, violence, and defensiveness."

LEARNING YOU CAN'T MEASURE EVERYTHING

Companies love to measure things. Just think how often you hear managers asking for metrics. Executives look for numbers that fit neatly in profit and loss columns. However, Sorge understands that there is no easy tool to tackle issues of culture.

"Often organizations are so focused on metrics that they ignore more systemic issues," he explains. "They figure if they can measure everything, it will be okay. However, often there are deeper cultural issues at play, and organizations are scared to confront those. Everyone may individually understand the problem, but the organization as a whole is unequipped to address it."

Without measurement, executives feel lost. Without numbers, there is no easy fix, no magic button to press. Instead, leaders are forced to turn to the individuals around them, a strategy they are all too reluctant to implement.

"People in the business world have trouble giving up control," Sorge says. "They always want more detail, more process. At the end of the day you need to be able to trust that the people around you are going to be able to get the job done, that they are going to help you." Too infrequently, people use their collective insights, wisdom, and judgment. They want to use quantitative test results as the decision maker. They need to see "the numbers" before deciding to take an action. Depending on people versus numbers will lead to a much higher likelihood of success.

FIGHTING FOR YOUR VALUES

We are comfortable with what we know and scared of what we don't. Even for Sorge, an individual who celebrates diversity, the unknown can be frightening.

"Behaviors and ideas that are out of the mainstream scare people," he says. "Sadly, if I don't do something, it is usually based on fear. It is hard for people to put themselves out there and describe how passionate they are about something. However, if you believe in something you have to communicate that. You don't need to over-explain, you just tell them what you are thinking about and why you are doing it. You will be surprised how often that is enough to convince people."

Values are something that we take with us everywhere. They are ideals that we believe in and that we fight for. However, Sorge feels no one should find themselves in a constant battle. "You need to find a place—whether it be your home, family, or organization that embodies the values that you hold," he says. "Otherwise, it will be hard to get through the days.

"I think passion is a huge value, because if you don't have it internally, your energy just runs out. You can only fake it for so long, I think. If you don't have passion, you are just going through the motions." It's the passion that also can join people together—it's the "bonding glue" that enables them to connect.

CONSTANTLY MOVING FORWARD

Moving together is difficult. It requires a unified vision and purpose. It requires a willingness to move with no guarantee of reaching the destination. It requires finding the common ground.

Sorge knows the tendency of businesses to hold fast to tradition, to stay with what has worked in the past. Organizations are so focused on how they got to where they are that they never define what they want to be.

"People don't move forward because they don't know what awaits them. They are scared," Sorge explains. "You have to be very clear what you are striving for, who you are, and who you are not. If your team has a common goal, it will be easier for individuals to join in and form a community. If your efforts are sporadic and disparate, you will not be able to motivate people."

OVERCOMING DISENGAGEMENT

"I think there is a big change in the business world today because people have seen so many companies let their employees down," Sorge says. "No one is immune to downsizing or relocation anymore. The reaction to this is that people are no longer turning to organizations as a source of continuity. People are not investing fully in their jobs or companies because they know it could all be gone tomorrow."

With constant downsizing and restructuring, today's companies make it easy for employees to disengage. Employees are unwilling to commit to an organization that is unwilling to commit to them. Loyalty has eroded. In the past, one identified himself to a stranger by explaining his work. People identify themselves differently today. Now identity has become more about who they are as a person.

"The increase of businesses letting people down is staggering," Sorge says. "People are not getting the fulfillment they need, and they are seeing other people equally unfulfilled. This generation saw a lot of families fall apart and now are questioning if that is what real life is all about. They saw it at home, now they are seeing people getting screwed at work. In their minds, it doesn't matter if they are the most gung ho person ever, the moment they don't need you, you are gone."

Great leaders recognize that they are not bound by societal norms; they can be catalysts for change. Movement is not easy—our prejudices can be powerful. However, the effort required for change will pay dividends for organizations willing to do the work.

MAKING THINGS HAPPEN FOR YOURSELF

"I had an uncle who was very nurturing," Sorge remembers. "He would never take no for an answer and would try anything. His motto was always 'If you do enough, enough will be successful.' You will fail at a lot, but you will be successful. I learned a lot from that kind of openness and strength, the idea that if it doesn't work, the world doesn't end. He believed that if you say it can work, then you can create it."

Determination is a powerful value in business. It can overcome the doubt, cynicism, and fear built into organizational cultures. Sorge understands that often the only restrictions we have are the ones we impose upon ourselves.

"I want to show people that what they want to have is totally possible, whatever it is," he says. "It is a matter of choice, and we choose our paths clearly and consciously. However, we must take personal responsibility for our actions. You can't blame others for your own failures. Your dreams are there for the taking, but they are not owed to you, you have to make them happen."

SEEING WHAT ISN'T THERE

Leaders listen. Leaders observe. Leaders demonstrate empathy.

"Understanding others involves not only paying attention to what they say, but also when they don't say anything at all," Sorge believes. "I have always been very emotionally intuitive and that is not easy. I think what happens is that you tend to take on people's fear and struggles. It allows for tremendous empathy, but also tremendous stress. I remember during speech class in seventh grade, some of the kids would go up there and be so nervous, and I would get tears in my eyes because I could feel their nervousness. I loved getting up and talking to people and giving a speech and I had no problem with it, but I would feel their pain profoundly."

Good leaders take on the problems of the team. They sense difficulties and put themselves not only in the minds, but also the hearts of those around them. This empathy allows them to develop meaningful solutions that impact people on a personal level.

One of the most commonly accepted clichés in business is the idea that talk is cheap; perhaps that is why executives are so free with their rhetoric and so hesitant with their actions. Great leaders exhibit a willingness to apply ideas, to stand behind their beliefs.

Sorge says, "So many people lack what I call applied awareness. You can give me all the awareness in the world, but you also have to be able to translate that into behavior. In corporate America, it is okay to talk about behavior, but difficult to get beyond talking. That level is not deep enough to make an impact. It allows people to feel like they are changing when they really are not. It is very superficial."

Great leaders demonstrate a consistent willingness to take action, to do what needs to be done to help an organization move forward. They are able to create their group action by forming teams where the individuals interact with each other based upon the discovery of common ground.

13

Step 5—Don't Take the Pleats Out

> "Everything is possible.
> If you want something, give something.
> When you make a choice, you change the future.
> Don't say no. Go with the flow.
> When you make a wish or express a desire, you plant a seed.
> Life is a journey. Enjoy every moment.
> You are here for a reason. Have fun discovering what it is."
>
> **DEEPAK CHOPRA**

Our fifth step is: Don't take the pleats out. It involves two initiatives: first, encourage creative ideas, and second, nurture professional passion. Leaving the pleats *in* means empowering people to express their inner feelings and creative thoughts, get engaged, be bold, and take risks. Taking the pleats *out* means remaining the same—plain, homogeneous, safe, and boring. Our mantra for this chapter is a call to establish strong convictions, communicate them emotionally, and not lose the fervor and professional passion for what you believe in and do daily.

LETTING CREATIVITY REIGN

Consider the way work all too often is: No one stands out in a group; most members follow the others; it is rare to see someone doing something differently.

How many times have you been in a group, had a creative idea, but didn't let it out, didn't raise your hand and share it? Perhaps this happens to you frequently or maybe you don't have any creative ideas anymore, because they are not really encouraged in the culture of your workplace. Maybe you are afraid to say it aloud for fear of being told it cannot work, or it has been tried before.

Now consider the way work could be: New ideas—even unusual ones—are highly encouraged and valued. Creative impulses are expressed and cultivated. After all, one employee's creative idea can turn a company or organization around.

How can creativity be nurtured at work? First, the leaders and managers have to want it. They have to want it for themselves, for each other, and for their organization. They must give their employees the freedom to take risks and play with ideas. This requires a new type of leader, one that encourages employees to connect with their creative potential and not take the pleats out!

Second, remember that creativity can be learned. It can even be taught in the workplace. Value intuition—it is the key to creativity. Simply put, intuition means letting go of our more structured, analytical mind. At the same time, it calls for a sense of trust in the abilities of our unconscious mind to organize experience, intuition, feelings, and gut reactions into something entirely new, even unanticipated. Intuition, then, involves learning to let go and stay open to ideas that surface unexpectedly.

If you knew that Thomas Edison had a contraption to capture wild ideas, would you try his method to snag them? We think so. According to Daniel Goleman, Paul Kaufman, and Michael Ray, authors of *The Creative Spirit,* Mr. Edison had a special napping chair. It was large, comfortable, and had good-sized arms rests. Before napping, he put ball bearings in his hands and two pie plates on the floor. He kept a notepad on his lap. Whenever he fell asleep the ball bearings would drop onto the pie plates and wake him up. He would jot down some notes on what was passing through his mind at the time, then fall back to sleep. This was his clever way to catch theta waves, brainwaves rich in creativity. Theta waves are full of silly, unusual, even bizarre ideas, and they often lead to fresh perceptions and thoughts. Adults can only experience these waves when dreams mix with reality, usually bordering a sleep state.

Imagine: The electric light bulb may have been discovered through the process of napping! Napping might be just fine in the workplace. Maybe creative impulses and new ideas would emerge if we were allowed to dose a little at our desks. Don't worry, bosses; employees won't need ball bearings and pie plates—their ringing phones will awaken them to creative ideas. Give them notepads or idea journals to encourage them to write down emerging ideas. If you really want to nurture more creativity, consider adding a comfortable couch to each office. Attach a clipboard or "think pad" to it. W. Clement Stone, the founder of Combined Insurance, used a bathtub, his "think tank," to generate new ideas, and he kept a small blackboard nearby to jot down his creative thoughts while relaxing in the tub.

So bosses, say, "Yes!" to creativity. Run out and buy everyone a "zany-thoughts journal," or an "innovative-solutions sofa" before employees want "bizarre-and-bold thoughts bathtubs" to generate new ideas. (Tubs are a lot harder to install anyway.) Embrace and encourage creative impulses. They could turn your workplace into something to shout about.

NURTURING PROFESSIONAL PASSION

Besides encouraging imaginative, inspired, and creative ideas, "don't take the pleats out" also translates into the following mantra: Maintain strong convictions, communicate them (emotionally, if necessary), and never lose your enthusiasm. We call it professional passion.

Scott Lutz, the former head of the General Mills-Dupont soy products joint venture, concurs: "Passionate people breathe passion into other people. Ultra-conservative, boring, connect-the-dots people spend money trying to take the pleats out of their lives, and don't energize people. You don't manufacture passion. But I look for passion. What I am trying to do is revolutionize business and make it great again, because big business for most people in corporate America has become dog-eat-dog and it sucks. I don't have any better way to say it. Even in companies where the stock price is doing well, people feel like they are shackled with a ball and chain."

Lutz understands that his philosophy requires an unorthodox approach to a staid and conservative business world. Most organizations value predictability and competition as a path to success. Lutz values passion.

Values-based leaders show a clear and strong conviction. They want to make a difference. This is not born out of conceit but rather a desire to share with others and do something significant. Lutz says, "I have a personal expectation to make a difference, to not just use up the air and the water on the planet. I believe I am here for a reason. I feel obliged to do something significant. I believe in that very strongly."

Values-based leaders are secure with themselves and comfortable expressing emotion. This means communicating their true feelings—being open enough with others so that positive praise, neutral dialogue, or constructive criticism can be freely conveyed. What is most electrifying is that leaders who display professional passion tend to give off charisma that excites and motivates others around them.

Professional passion means having the opportunity to engage in something that one truly loves to do in the workplace. There is a key prerequisite. It requires a cultural environment that nurtures this freedom. Imagine this: After considerable soul-searching, a person discovers what he or she wants to do within an organization, and then learns that the culture of that workplace says "no." The norms and values of that company dictate that one cannot express personal interests, enthusiasms, or even knowledge. Sadly, one finds such restrictive cultures in many work settings.

If professional passion exists, a different mandate is presented. Employees experience the freedom to pursue their professional desires, interests, and skills, applying them to numerous opportunities and problems encountered within the workplace. When the culture is not prohibitive, work becomes an act of creative professional expression.

In this chapter, each of our three interviewees tried to do revolutionary things. Each was not afraid of the unknown; in fact, they saw it as an opportunity for their future work. The first, Leon Despres, is a public servant; the second, Robin Gilman, is a former R & D scientist, turned communication consultant; and the third, Scott Lutz, the source of our chapter title, is an innovative businessman. They each provide the inspiration, judgment, vision, and importantly, professional passion from which to fashion a better future.

••

Passionate about Politics

Leon Despres
Former Chicago alderman (now deceased)

At 98, Leon Despres was trim, lively and lucid. In 2005, he published his own memoir. He has been entwined in and impassioned by Chicago politics for five decades.

Despres was elected to the city council to represent Hyde Park and Woodlawn as fifth ward alderman in 1955. That same year, Richard J. Daley, his chief adversary, was elected mayor. One of the few reform-minded independents, he was a strong leader within the group of 50 city alderman. When cronyism and corruption defined Chicago politics, his progressive efforts often faced 49 to one thrashings in the city council. As a lone voice, he persevered and became known as the figure that could turn the mayor's face various shades of red with rage. Mr. Despres recalls the political tactics used to keep him quiet during meetings. "My microphone was cut off as I was talking," he remembers. "Or adversaries deliberately interrupted me with a point of order in city council meetings." Despite these combative tactics, Mr. Despres shepherded 20 years of improvements as a city alderman, challenging the Democratic political machine at every turn. Later, he worked as a parliamentarian for the Jane Byrne and Harold Washington administrations, successors to the Daley administration, and as an attorney, lecturer, and teacher.

Mr. Despres was an unwavering maverick. He always stood tall, earnest, and alone, talking back to those who lusted for political power. He spoke up and stood up not only for housing desegregation and the saving of historic buildings (his two favorite causes), but also for civil and human rights, and opportunities for women. Facing long and difficult odds, he took up the fights that needed to be fought. He confronted and championed causes, always doing what he felt was right, regardless of the political price. He had unparalleled professional passion for politics for most of his long life.

• •

Early Influences

Despres' father was a small clothing manufacturer who inspired strong social values in his son. His family kept many books in their home, and his father read works such as Booker T. Washington's *Up From Slavery* at an early age.

Before his 11th birthday, however, Leon's father died. His mother raised him and his sister alone on a small income. A local rabbi, Abel Hirsh, became Despres' new role model. Hirsh had a strong positive influence on his development, and these early religious influences reinforced his Judaism. When Despres was 14, his mother took the two children to Europe where he studied at a French high school. Today, he speaks five languages.

His father demonstrated a devotion to public service and imparted upon Despres the will to do what is right for the people, rather than to be a politician.

"If I want to run for office, I need to *do* something first—help advance a cause or show personal commitment and activity," Despres says. "You cannot start by focusing on getting elected. You have to start with a passionate belief in something." He feels that John Adams and Harry Truman were two American leaders and politicians who had unlimited devotion to serving the public interest. His thoughts serve as an ideal guide for any newcomer to the political arena: "Great politicians really want to serve their public. They recognize the need to help make their societies better. Strong leaders demonstrate a willingness to listen. They also surround themselves with people who are greater than they are. They need to be fair with everyone."

Passion for Service

In a public life spanning many years of service, Despres is most proud of his assaults on patterns of racial discrimination. His passion for inclusiveness is unparalleled. Although he is white, he was known for years as "the lone Negro on the City Council." When African-American aldermen allied with Mayor Daley and were silent on housing desegregation at the time, Despres single-handedly took up the cause. Besides this focus on equal opportunity, his second biggest achievement, in his view, was working for architectural preservation, what he calls "the hallmark of Chicago today."

Despres conveys an urgent request to young people: "Stand for something and then act on it—do something rather than just talk about the things you don't like." He stresses that we need to have vibrant young people to keep up interest and activity in pubic affairs. "So much can be done when people are active," he attests. "That doesn't mean you have to run for office. There are all kinds of social and public interest groups and activities that can make a huge contribution to humanity." He wants to pass on the torch now to those like him, who have creative ideas and professional passion, those, like him, who won't take their pleats out.

Passionate about Communication

Robin Gilman
Scientific and communications consultant, Wrigley Global Innovation Center

After spending 15 years at Warner Lambert as an R & D scientist, Robin Gilman decided it was time to help people communicate more effectively and passionately. "Most business dialogue is a bunch of dribble or, at the very best, emotionless, one-way monologues," he says. He wanted to change that. He saw the need for people to get excited when they attended a business presentation, not fall asleep. He wanted to awaken their senses.

Gilman decided to start his own innovation and communications consulting firm, which was focused on making business meetings more exciting and meaningful by increasing the impact and clarity of the communications. Gilman possesses an extraordinary ability to transform ideas and concepts into visual elements. From these mental images, he creates powerful, audience-sensitive media and events to effectively communicate important messages. Currently, he is solidly booked but spends a lot of his time helping Surinder Kumar, the Chief Innovation Officer at Wrigley, make innovation understood and recognized by the company's employees.

Passion for Expression

Gilman's values stemmed largely from his mother, who strongly believed that there was nothing in the world you couldn't achieve. As Robin shares, "This tenacious belief, that the world really is your oyster, enabled me to feel free to pursue whatever I wanted."

The inner passion that Gilman possesses came from his fervent values structure that gave him a love of life and perspective that a person has to make the best of life everyday. He says proudly, "I'm happy with the values I have and the person I've become."

His mother was outgoing; his dad was passive. He was an only child and realized at an early age that you get things to happen when you talk openly rather than being passive and quiet. At the center of success, is his view about open and expressive communications. He believes in creating an open environment where, as he says, "Two-way communication, both up and down the organization, becomes the norm—not the exception." This is the grease and the glue that keeps an organization lubricated, on one hand, and cohesive and bonded together on the other. Gilman sees great value in open systems where people can be self-organizing. In these types of environments, he says, "Energy can flow in and out and around; similar to nature, there is a natural sense of order that results."

Listening and Flexibility

Gilman's major life divining rod is to seek understanding by listening to others rather than telling others how it is. His other guiding principle is flexibility and openness. "Even in a business context, develop a suite of solutions—not just one," he states. "If you have multiple, well-thought out solutions in front of you, that's what provides the flexibility to examine and pick the best one. Too often, managers only pick one solution and spend all of their time trying to persuade and convince others on the merits of that one alternative—and only that one. That type of rigidity does nobody any good in an organization."

Catalyst for Change

In order for change to occur, people need to see a reason to shift their current behavior. It is so much easier to accept the status quo. Gilman says, "Often we need to reach a certain height of dissatisfaction before we are willing or motivated to change. That's why change occurs in a nonlinear way—it rambles and meanders for years, and then it accelerates into rapid high gear, and then change occurs."

Gilman's view of change is similar to our own—and that's why we feel that a new leadership archetype is needed today. People have reached a high level of dissatisfaction with the control-and-compete model of leadership and want to see change now.

INDIVIDUALS—THE HUB OF THE TEAM

"Developing strong individuals is the key ingredient for high-performing teams," Gilman says. "We need to address issues on an individual-by-individual basis in order to have team effectiveness." He believes that if people have individual issues on the inside, then they will cause issues outside to surface and impact their team. Eventually, a person's issues surface, and the team has to play psychologist for that individual—and that's not fair to the team.

Gilman has seen a lot of leadership training on diversity, but, according to him, most companies take an approach of embracing diversity that fails to focus on the individual. "It's all about how you are with other people; it's all about the individual and how you treat them," he says. "That's why creating a common language and developing active listening skills is so important for fostering effective one-to-one dialogue."

In 2020, Gilman sees a closer world. "People will be more integrated with each other," he imagines. "They will be more interested in doing the right things for each other, their countries, and the environment overall." He also envisions more of a 'win-win' focus when making deals with folks—it just doesn't make sense in the long run for two people to create a win-lose situation for themselves.

One of his strongly held beliefs is: "Let's find something that we both can smile about." Gilman is a vocal and opinionated advocate for finding the common position between two people's differing points of view. He espouses: "Let's just find the intersecting and overlapping point so that we can focus on it instead of on the extremities."

"You can't squeeze water," he says with a wry smile. Likewise, his leadership philosophy is well captured in his description of the Chinese finger toy. "You know that bamboo tubular toy that you stick your two fingers into each end of it and your fingers get caught in it? Only when you relax your fingers and actually push them both together will the toy release—so you can remove your two index fingers from the two ends."

The same is true with leadership. "We need to have fluidity and looseness within organizations—a communications ebb and flow—back and forth. Not tightness and constraint—that just won't work," he says. "Leadership is all about creating a place where you can sit down and talk with someone."

Passionate about Business Innovation

Scott Lutz
CEO and President,
Grocery Shopping
Network, Inc.

"There was a teacher I had in eighth grade who had a profound impact on me," says Scott Lutz. "Once, we were debating in his class and I won the argument and in the process totally humiliated this other person. I was feeling pretty good about myself, and I remember he pulled me aside and said, 'Scott, you know I am really disappointed in you.' He made me realize that it wasn't just about winning, but how you won and how you carried yourself. He made me realize that you have to choose what to do with your intellect and talent."

Thirty years later, sporting a goatee and dressed like he is about to hit the golf course, Scott Lutz does not look like your average corporate executive. His seemingly boundless enthusiasm and disdain for bureaucracy are more suited for a precocious teenager than a business leader. Yet few individuals have as impressive of a record of producing innovative products in the food and beverage industry as Lutz.

"I think that a lot of people in business are one person in every other walk of their life, and then professionally, they somehow turn on a button and behave differently," he says. "I think that's a recipe for a personal disaster, but I also think it leads to a level of insincerity, and it is just a matter of time before people figure it out."

OPENING NEW DOORS TO SEE THE FUTURE

Lutz says, "I value the ability to creatively derive a way to find a solution, instead of memorizing or just re-applying the same old idea to solve a problem. I am not a big believer that one-size-fits-all. I think that is the difference between living in the moment and focusing on the future. When you are able to figure out an innovative solution, derived from the information that you have, then you open a door to the future."

The value of what exists is already defined; it is limited and replicable. Sure, it is easier to take what has already been done and try to fit it into a new situation, but then you are bound by the constraints of a soon-to-be outdated tool.

Lutz recognizes that in order to grow for the future, you need to think beyond what already exists. Great leaders don't dwell as much on what they have. Instead they look at what they don't have and how they can meet that demand.

"I believe life is all about opening doors," he says. "Part of that is opening new doors. You go down an alleyway, there's a door at the end, you don't know what's in it, but you are not afraid to open it. A lot of times there is nothing in it. Sometimes there is scary stuff in it, and occasionally, there's a real pearl in it. I do that with my friends and I do that with my kids. I try to do pioneering things all the time. Part of it is that I just try to put myself in situations where I have no choice but to resourcefully respond and react."

Most people are scared of the unknown. For leaders like Lutz, however, the unknown represents opportunity; it represents the future. While others shy away, Lutz runs toward the door, anxious to be the first one through it.

FOCUSING ON YOUR PERSONAL GREATNESS

Several years ago, Lutz's wife was diagnosed with breast cancer. They didn't know how serious it was or what was going to be required for treatment. At the same time, he was in the midst of leading a start-up company and going to market with a new product. While he needed to provide support for his wife, he also didn't feel like he could ignore things at work.

"During that time, I found that leaning on my values was invigorating, that I didn't have to shut down in every area because by focusing on my values I could hit on the most critical things with my wife's situation and at work. I found myself relying more and more on the things that I did naturally well."

Our values allow us to distill things and focus on what is really important. In this way we are able to maximize our strengths. For Lutz, turning to his values provided him the channel to satisfy seemingly competing demands. Personal values are not picked from a book or pulled from thin air; they reflect our personalities and behaviors. As such, reliance on our values allows us to perform more effectively.

"More and more I believe in working on what you are passionate about. I believe that talented people are somewhat cursed in that they can be quite good at a lot of things, but many of which they don't care about, some of which they probably don't even like. But I think you make the most difference with your time on this planet doing more of what you are great at versus what you are good at."

DEALING WITH PEOPLE

Lutz knows he is not a typical corporate executive. In fact, it is something he celebrates. He also knows that not everyone welcomes his attitude. Often he must fight for what he believes. It is a battle worth fighting, however, because with victory comes results.

"People who work with me see a guy come in with a free-flowing, energetic, passionate personality," he says. "They see a person who is not afraid to wear a goatee, who rarely wears ultra-nice clothing, a person who relies heavily on his ideas versus his position. I try to reach down into the organization. I like to deal directly with people. I don't have meetings in my office where I am sitting behind the big part of the table and 12 people are crammed on the other side. I like to meet people on their turf. I want people to know me with all my little warts. I find that has a real impact on morale. People are excited to work with people that they have access to—who share their hopes and fears and listen to them."

There is no single management style that works with everyone. Lutz recognizes that the more you treat people as individuals, the more successful you will be. Values are uncompromising, but the way in which you convey them to other people can—and should—vary.

"I'm a big believer that your leadership changes with each person that you deal with, and I don't believe that I can manage 20 people all the same way," Lutz says. "I have some principles that I try to hold to, but certain people need more room; certain people need less room."

VALUING PROGRESS OVER RESULTS

Results—everyone in business wants them. They measure, benchmark, and set deadlines. However, with this focus on the end result, the journey along the way is often forgotten.

"One of the biggest things I look for is a sense of making progress," Lutz says. "I think too often people say, 'I want to get from A to Z and if I'm not at L by this date, then I'm a failure.' The reality is our eyes are always bigger than our stomachs when we have goals. The main thing is, 'Am I getting better?'"

Leaders understand that if an organization is learning and a team is growing, then there is no true failure, regardless of the results. For great leaders a number or date does not simply define a failure; it is defined by an attitude of defeat, an unwillingness to keep tackling problems. Lutz understands that the more important goal is progress, because over time progress is the only thing that will consistently deliver results—and results occur when creative ideas are encouraged and professional passion is expressed. So please don't take the pleats out!

14

Step 6— Root for People

"Sis Boom Bah! Rah rah rah!"
the oldest football massed cheer recorded at football games in the United States

"And it's root, root, root for the home team; if they don't win it's a shame."
cheer at a baseball game

Good leaders know that it's critical to keep the group alive and open, share ideas, convey warmth and interest, identify and address members' needs, and apply knowledge to help them grow, rally together, and cheer for others. Our sixth step is: Root for people.

Consider this scene: The boss never cheers for anyone. He is mean and difficult. Subordinates are "tied" to their desks, each wearing the customary corporate uniform: black suit, white shirt, and red tie. They are neatly paired into identical cubicles, and no communication is allowed.

More than any other factor, the boss determines the culture of the workplace. Many bosses are command-and-control types. Their organizations, for better or worse, follow controlled objectives. Check out your boss. If he or she has the following characteristics, then you work for a "control guy": gives orders, disciplines, likes hierarchy, has or wants all the answers, demands respect, interested in the bottom line, focuses on limits, issues action-plans, is strict, and constantly keeps employees on their toes.

Now, consider another kind of boss: He or she roots for others and uses cheers to encourage and accomplish tasks. The following list will help identify the traits of this facilitate-and-cheer boss: Empowers, serves as a role model, acts as an agent for change, connects or networks, facilitates, rewards, encourages speaking out, motivates, nurtures creativity, serves, seeks vision, relates salary to performance, uses a teaching and rooting-for archetype, encourages mentoring, nourishes growth, asks questions, and reaches out.

Bosses usually fit into one of these two categories. The control-and-command boss is rigid, impersonal, closed off, mechanistic, located in the corner office, and has little time for others. This boss rarely roots for people. The cheering boss is flexible, personal, open, and holistic, finds time for others, and *always* roots for people. This boss wants employees to develop their potential, become the best that they can become, and build a caring team.

CHEERING OTHERS ON

Football fans often chant *"Sis Boom Bah! Rah rah rah!"* It is a cheer to encourage the team. The English word "hurrah" was preceded by *huzza,* a word used by sailors, and generally connected to *heeze* or to hoist, which was the cry that sailors made when hoisting or hauling. Today, "hurray" means to shout encouragement or to applaud. Picture your workplace as a sailing ship with employees chanting together as they encourage each other to do their work.

Two of our interviewees, Congresswoman Jan Schakowsky and Master Chief Petty Officer of the Coast Guard Vincent Patton, depict two different ways to root for people. Both of their lives are connected to the idea of serving others in their respective "communities." They share a profound and far-reaching effort to root for people—all the time and at every turn. There is no divided effort here. While on the surface we may hear them cheer others on, their love of people authentically permeates their work. They look out for others, and are encouraging, advancing, and promoting. Schakowsky is an advocate for women, ordinary people, the forgotten, unpopular causes, and citizens who lack prestige and clout to lobby on their own. Patton looks for the good and praises it, tries to understand and respect different viewpoints, strives to align individual and team interests, embraces diversity, builds on individual strengths, and wants to touch and improve the lives of others. They root for the people around them.

Encouraging Women

Jan Schakowsky
U.S. Congresswoman

Of the 540 members of the 110th United States Congress, only 90 representatives are women. In 2007, only eleven Fortune 500 companies had female CEOs. Jan Schakowsky understands that as a powerful female, she is constantly under the microscope—it is a role she embraces.

Clearly, Schakowsky encourages and roots for women.

"I feel that part of my mission is to encourage young women to see being a member of Congress as an attainable goal," she says. "I want to empower them to follow their dreams and envision themselves as the person at the top. I think it is important for women who achieve these roles to reach back and give a helping hand to others. I think we need to continue to make a stink about the lack of opportunities for women, to keep pushing, pushing and organizing. There are plenty of women out there thirsting for opportunities."

SERVING THE ORDINARY

Schakowsky roots for ordinary people. "My public service and activism is guided by the notion that our society can be more responsive to the needs of ordinary people in every way," she says. "The opportunities in our country are rich because of our wealth and talent. We have the resources to shape the world in a really positive way, and that's what government and public service are about to me. I want to influence change for ordinary people."

Schakowsky gives voice to the individuals who lack the strength to shout above the noise of politics. She fights for the poor, the uninsured, the elderly, and the abused. In a world where elected officials always have the next campaign in mind, Schakowsky supports the rights of immigrants and children—groups that cannot even cast a ballot.

She says, "I think that the challenge of this new century and the real destabilizing threats in the world have to do with this incredible imbalance of wealth, the inequities that we face. This contrast of incredible wealth and overwhelming poverty cannot be maintained."

EMPOWERING HOUSEWIVES

Schakowsky began her political activism in 1969, as a young housewife in the northwest suburbs of Chicago. At the time there were no freshness dates on food packages; everything was coded. "We were all trying to decode numbers on packages to determine how old the food was," says Schakowsky. For example, a series of numbers on milk had to be added up in a certain way to tell the date and the month of its freshness period, and the color of the twist tie on bread indicated how old it was. Frustrated, Schakowsky and six girlfriends formed National Consumers United (NCU), a group dedicated to putting freshness dates on food. Schakowsky and her neighbors had no idea where to start, only that the system was not right.

The housewives would question the store employees and demand to know the rotation of the old food. They translated thousands of food codes so people could figure out if the food was fresh, eventually publishing a NCU codebook. In twos and threes they would scour the aisles of stores, carrying clipboards to record information. Eventually, the companies caved to the pressure.

"It was such an empowering experience," Schakowsky says. "It changed my life and my perception of myself as someone who could affect change. I realized we could do something, just little old me and my friends. We could make something visible. And in fact, I have to tell you that even now when the legislative process is so grinding, I will just hang out in the dairy section and watch people check freshness dates."

Sometimes problems can seem too simple or meaningless as to be unworthy of treatment. It is always easier to accept the status quo, or to view it as someone else's problem. Schakowsky understood that passivity would accomplish nothing. Her actions were not motivated by a desire for financial gain or recognition. She was driven by a core need to right a wrong.

"I was on a mission thinking, 'Okay, we did this, what else can we do? Let's figure out what other changes need to be made,'" she says. "In the process I saw who the decision makers were and thought, first of all, I could do the job they were doing, but beyond that I would bring to it a certain passion for making these kinds of changes."

GIVING VOICE TO THE FORGOTTEN

Shortly after being elected to Congress, Schakowsky started receiving dozens of calls from immigrants complaining about poor services in Chicago. Customers would wait for hours in line at the Immigration and Naturalization Services office, only to be turned away when officials had filled their daily quota. The immigrants were scared to confront the INS out of fear of jeopardizing their relationships with the agency.

Schakowsky realized something needed to be done to call attention to this problem. She went down to the INS office and joined the thousands of people waiting in a line stretching around the block. After waiting for more than three and a half hours, a staff member came out and said they had reached their limit and were done seeing people for the day. When Schakowsky refused to leave, the staff member threatened to call the police.

A week later, Schakowsky returned with the media in tow. The INS line was gone in two weeks.

"It is not enough to be in a position of power," she says. "You have to show real leadership. You need to be somebody who has a little *umph* to them, to use your office to explore the boundaries. You have to say, 'We have this little beachhead of power, how do we exploit this office to empower people, to make change, to help organize.'"

WILLING TO LEAD

Leadership requires tough decisions. Not everyone is going to be happy all the time. Schakowsky knows that she cannot please all of her constituents with every vote; however, she never backs down from an unpopular decision. This voluntary accountability forces her to think through her positions.

"There is a common saying on Capitol Hill that, 'If you have to explain it, it is a bad vote,'" she says. "Now think about that for a minute. That means that you can't lead. If you aren't willing to take a position you might have to explain, then you can only try and figure out where people are and follow. This is all too common. The philosophy is that if you can't do it in a sound bite, then it is too risky."

Several years ago, Schakowsky was invited to a business conference in Bangalore, India, where she sat on a panel discussing the role of government. An Indian government official mentioned that he did not believe labor and environmental rights should be part of core trade agreements. Schakowsky disagreed vehemently, arguing that economic justice was not a sidebar to globalization, but had to be an integral part of it.

She sat there surrounded by foreign politicians, in the high-tech capital of the region, and voiced a highly unpopular view. After the panel, the South African minister said he thought her comments were gutsy. For Schakowsky it was nothing extraordinary—it was simply what she believed.

"I am lucky that I represent a district that allows me to be an advocate for unpopular causes and not worry about campaigning all the time," she says. "I think there is a hunger out there for people who will just tell the truth, who won't trim and duck and dodge. Politicians are so worried about figuring out the best, measured way to do things. And anyone who doesn't think that money influences policy is being ridiculous. It is absolutely shameful what a dominant force it is; there is no doubt about it."

TAKING A BROADER VIEW

Schakowsky serves as an advocate on a wide range of issues ranging from universal health care to identity theft. However, her work is unified by her mission of serving ordinary citizens—individuals that lack the prestige and political clout to lobby on their own behalf. Schakowsky does not pick issues based on the level of support they garner, rather she is guided by her personal judgment of what is right.

She says, "Martin Luther King had a tremendous influence on me. But one of the things I really admire about Dr. King is that many people advised him not to take a position on the Vietnam War. They said, 'Here's your niche; here's your issue; you are working on the civil rights issue and this will cut into your base of support; it will distract you from your mission, and don't do that.' Instead he took a much broader view that was completely consistent with his social agenda. That was a large risk on his part. And when he made his decision, he didn't just make a speech, he came out completely opposed to the war."

Great leaders are often viewed as risk takers, people who violate norms. However, often for the leaders themselves, the greater risk would be to stay the course and violate their personal values. Decision making can be easy when leaders support, root for, and serve others.

Valuing People First

Vincent Patton
Retired Master Chief Petty Officer of the Coast Guard

"I live my life by the values of People, Passion, and Performance. That is my personal philosophy. That is what I share with others," said Master Chief Petty Officer of the Coast Guard Vincent W. Patton III. He never planned on joining the Coast Guard. He wanted to be a navy man, just like his oldest brother. The walls of his room were covered with posters and banners featuring fighter planes and navy blue.

When he turned seventeen, he had his father drive him downtown to the recruiting office so he could sign up to begin service right after high school. Patton spotted a man in a blue sailor suit and ran to his office. Only after sitting down did he notice the gentleman's hat read "U.S. Coast Guard." Too embarrassed to leave, Patton listened to the man describe the service and liked what he heard.

Patton had always said he wanted to join the navy, but never thought about why; he just wanted to be like his brother. However, the Coast Guard promoted individuality and focused on humanitarian service, two ideals that appealed to Patton. He expressed this new interest to his parents, and his father was not very enthusiastic. Patton's father was worried that the Coast Guard would be a difficult place for an African-American.

However, his mother looked at him and said, "I don't know much about the Coast Guard, only what you told me. But if it's the issue that there are so few minorities in the Coast Guard at this time, it will never change unless people go in and make that change. You have been living your brother's life for a long time and it's time for you to live your own life, and if going in the Coast Guard is the way for you to live your own life that's what you should do. You will be able to handle anything, and you will be able to make something of yourself."

Patton went on to become the service's first African-American Master Chief Petty Officer of the Coast Guard, proving the wisdom of his mother.

REMEMBERING WHERE YOU COME FROM

In 1976, Patton was on recruiting duty in Chicago and met a man named Alex Haley, who introduced himself as a retired U.S. Coast Guard Chief Petty Officer. As African-Americans in a Caucasian dominated organization, the two shared a common bond and quickly struck up a friendship. It was later that day that Patton learned Haley was also a writer, and had penned *The Autobiography of Malcolm X* and *Roots*. Soon after, Patton sat down to read *Roots*, which helped open his eyes to the value of history.

"He [Haley] helped me realize the importance of learning about where you come from, how that helps you develop character," Patton says. "You need to embrace family history, heritage, and traditions. These things teach you values."

Haley was fond of an old biblical saying that resonated with Patton: "Find the good and praise it." As Patton progressed in his career, and met individuals filled with prejudices and ignorance, he always tried to remember that ideal.

"You need to seek out the good in people," he says. "You need to work closely to bring people to an understanding of what those successes are."

LOVING PEOPLE

Every business is different. They have different products and locations; they have varied offices and benefits. The one constant is the people—there is no avoiding them. They are your colleagues, your bosses, and your customers.

"My life's mission is working with people," Patton says. "That's what I am good at and that is what I love to do. People ask me, 'What do you love most about your job?' It's the people. 'What do I love most about life?' It's the people. I love people. I love talking about people, I love learning about people. I love not trying to change people, but getting them to understand my point of view and having me understand theirs, so that we respect each other."

While certain positions may require technical or product expertise, leadership requires one to be an expert in people. "It's a great ego-builder to be told by a number of people that you could make a ton of money, but there's no value I can place on what I have with the love of people," Patton says.

SEEKING MEANING NOT MENTIONS

"When you think about how you can make the best impact on this earth, it is not a question of wanting to be on the front page of every newspaper or anything like that," Patton says. "My thrill has always been with just seeing one or two people that I have come across be successful. That's what I want to continue to do."

There is a significant difference between attention and impact. Having your name on the marquee is meaningless if it is forgotten tomorrow. Great leaders touch the lives of those they work with. They are not a title to be feared or avoided; rather they engage themselves with their team. When it comes to relationships, great leaders will take quality over quantity any day.

"I don't think I can change the world by myself, but I think I can at least be an instrument to chip away a little bit to make society better," Patton says. "That's what I am on this earth for."

SEEING THE DOMINO EFFECT

The interconnected nature of teams is both a strength and a danger to an organization. Leaders recognize that no decision occurs in isolation, and something that seems innocuous to you can be significant to a colleague.

"I like to try to get people to understand ethics, to understand what doing the right thing means," Patton says. "There is only one way of doing the right thing. You have to be concerned about the impact of your decisions on the people around you. Actions have a domino effect, and sometimes you think you have done the right thing in terms of yourself, and all of a sudden it hurts someone else along the way."

Although there is only one way to do the right thing, it is rarely the easy way. Patton suggests instead of looking at what a decision does for you, focus on what it can do for others.

"I think the right approach in terms of defining and doing the right thing is always taking a step back and recognizing what your decision or what your action is, finding where it positively impacts others," he says. "Look at what you do, what you say, how you do it and ask if you can see how it has a positive impact on others."

CULTIVATING YOUR IMAGINATION

Patton may be a disciplined military man, but his office is an inviting mess. Toys, books, and papers are strewn about. Yet there is a method to his madness. Everything represents something; every item has a purpose.

"I have a 40-year-old piece of Silly Putty," he says. "Know why I have it here? I am from a large family and on Christmas we all got one thing. When I was seven years old all I got was Silly Putty. When I went to school, everyone would go through what they got and they would get to me and all I had was the Silly Putty. But you know what? I was the happiest kid in the class with just my Silly Putty. I found a bazillion things to do with it. I formulated a wonderful imagination as a child because we didn't have a lot of physical things, but I had imagination, as did the rest of my brothers and sisters."

Patton has more than 100 navy blue baseball caps from Coast Guard members across the country; he keeps them all. He has toys that symbolize strength (a spinach-eating Popeye), diversity (a frog-green Kermit), flexibility (his trusty horse Pokey) and other values. The items are not expensive, but you cannot put a price on memories and meaning. They all capture his love for people, and his top priority of rooting for them.

EMBRACING SELFISHNESS

Selfishness can be a powerful tool if put in its proper context. Leaders should seek individuals that want to succeed, that want to build their individual strengths.

"There has to be a split decision on individual and team," Patton says. "I am a subscriber to the 'What's in it for me?' statement. I feel that leaders today feel very frustrated in dealing with people who have a 'What's in it for me attitude?' I think that when you take individuals and work with them to build their strengths, that's how you tie in the team effort. You approach the team as individuals first where everyone has separate strengths, then mesh them together so they can all work collectively."

The challenge for leaders is to align individual and team interests. They need to convince individuals that it is in their best interests for the team to succeed.

PROMOTING VOCATIONAL DIVERSITY

The job climate has changed dramatically over the past several decades. Gone are the days of individuals staying with an organization for a lifetime. Today's generation takes a different perspective toward the idea of a career.

"I think we are coming into a cultural evolution," Patton says. "Complacency has a different definition then what it did 20 years ago. It used to be that someone would stay with the same organization for 30 years. Now we are beginning to see that maybe it isn't so bad to be able to develop a skill set and then tuck it away and move on and do something else. It used to be we looked to climb a traditional ladder. Now, people are more inclined to take the monkey bars, because we are not comfortable or happy unless we are able to try different things."

Formerly, people strived to become an expert in one area. Today, individuals seek to develop an arsenal of expertise. Strong leaders will recognize the value of versatile individuals. In a rapidly changing business world, leaders will design teams that can easily adapt.

"I think what organizations are going to have to do, if they aren't already, is to be open-minded, to promote vocational diversity," Patton says. "Every large organization is just the total of smaller organizations. I think organizations need to give employees freedom and flexibility to explore different functions within the company, to see how everything is interconnected."

People do not become complacent on their own. Complacency is borne out of an environment that fails to challenge an individual. Great leaders empower the individuals around them and keep them engaged.

"People don't jump ship to the competition because they are disloyal or they dislike their boss," Patton says. "They go to the competition because the competition has something a little different, a little bit out of the mainstream. They are tired of the same old thing and want a new opportunity. It is not that they dislike their work, they just can't wear these pants anymore and they have got to go for another size."

BECOMING A CHEERLEADER

"I think if there is anything to define the job of a leader, it is the job of chief cheerleader of the organization," Patton says. "You have to be the salesman of the company philosophy. But first of all, you have got to believe it yourself and you have got to be able to take what you can believe in and be able to turn it out."

There will be times when you will do everything asked of you, and you will do everything you intended, and things will still go wrong. Patton believes it is in those moments when it is most important to stay true to your values.

"I believe in the idea that adversity breeds inspiration," he says. "You have some knockdowns in your life—you get your heart broken or lose a job, and then for a while you get tired of feeling bad. You can only go through that 'woe is me' attitude for so long, and now you want to do something about yourself, and you find something to be able to work your way out of that rut again. I try to use situations that didn't go well to determine how I might make it right. It's important to look for that winning situation."

FIGHTING FIRE WITH WATER

Early in his career, Patton worked as a radioman for a chief who was racist. He called Patton a baboon and called him stupid. Patton took it all and fulfilled his duty. During that stint, there was an emergency that required Patton to relay medical information on the Morse code circuit. He sat by the radio for more than 18 hours, communicating information that saved the life of a crewman.

When they left the ship, the chief, who had been filled with so much hatred towards Patton, introduced him to his wife and kids as "the best radioman on the ship."

"My mother taught me a long time ago that you never fight fire with fire, you fight fire with water," Patton says. "If someone treats you bad, you don't treat him or her bad. You have to be able to turn the other cheek and rouse within yourself the strength to carry on."

Throughout our interviews, rooting for people emerged as a critical step in building a culture with a high performance, caring team. Cheers motivate people. It is as simple as that. We hope you recognize the unmistakable power of encouragement, representing the needs of others, and serving people.

15

Step 7—Leave Some Money on the Table

> *"Not everything that can be counted counts,
> and not everything that counts can be counted."*
>
> **ALBERT EINSTEIN**

> *"My grandfather worked in a refinery and was offered
> some fairly significant dollars for black lung and said,
> 'I absolutely will not accept those dollars. This company gave
> me a job when I needed a job to raise my family and
> that's all that they are responsible for.' He taught me the
> idea of not taking something that you don't deserve or that
> you haven't earned in some way."*
>
> **JERRY FISHER, retired VP of Corporate R & D at Baxter Healthcare**

Suggest to a business executive that they take a deal offering less money and you will likely be laughed out of the room. There is usually too much emphasis placed on making the most profitable decision, and not enough thought given to making the *right* decision. "We need to leave some money on the table," says Dipak Jain, dean of Kellogg School of Management. Always negotiating for the last cent or jockeying for the best position or project does not always yield the greatest results in the long run.

Leaving $1 Million on the Table

Henry Givray
Chairman, President, and
CEO of SmithBucklin

Henry S. Givray, Chairman and CEO of SmithBucklin Corporation, the world's largest association management company, left something on the table more than once. The story of the first time he did so, which he has never told to anyone outside of a small number of close colleagues, family members, and friends, will leave your eyes wide open.

Givray served as CEO of a successful online legal services start-up for four years that spanned both the dot-com boom and bust periods. In 2001, after the bottom fell out of the financial markets and it was clear that it would be difficult to take the company public, Givray negotiated a deal in which LexisNexis would acquire the company. "We agreed on a price of $68.7 million, but when the deal term sheet came to us it stipulated that $1 million of it was to go directly to me," he says. The buyer believed that the $1 million would help ensure Givray employed his full commitment, energy, enthusiasm, and selling capabilities to make the transaction a reality.

The board of Givray's company recognized his accomplishments, so they approved the million dollars. His executive team said, "Henry, you deserve this." However, Givray knew that the $1 million was coming at the expense of the other shareholders, those who believed in the company—and him. Also, the president of LexisNexis didn't understand that Givray was not necessarily motivated by money. Givray says: "Of course I was going to give my heart and soul to make the deal happen. It was the right thing to do; it was right for our employees, and given what was going on in the financial markets it was a phenomenal deal. I remember we had a late night board meeting where the board unanimously approved the deal, including the $1 million for me. I went home that night, and it just didn't feel right. First, it put the board in a bad position. In effect, it put a gun to their heads. Second, it was taking away from other shareholders. And third, the reason behind it was to make sure that I was going to be motivated and energized, which was all wrong."

The next morning Givray announced he was giving back the $1 million.

••

"Everyone was shocked," he says. "It's not as if I was going to make millions through stock options and was giving back one. Because of dilution and the collapse of the financial markets, my stock options were worthless and frankly, I was at a low point in terms of my financial assets. One person said to me, 'No one is going to remember this after the deal is done.' My answer was, 'Yeah, but I would remember forever. If I don't give the money back, I'd have to live with the fact that I had not been true to my values.' And you know what? I don't regret giving back the money one bit. My wife was a little taken aback at first, but after we talked she completely understood and supported the move as I knew she would. I neither expected, nor did I get, any 'bonus points' for it either. As customary in these types of transactions, our board did award me a monetary bonus after the deal was done, though much more modest than the LexisNexis offer. Nevertheless, I instructed the board to use some of that bonus to award other members of my management team. I did what felt right, and it was really easy for me because I have always believed that doing things that are right is a much more powerful guide than doing things to derive a specific reward."

CONNECTING TO YOUR VALUES

"Over the years I've concluded that the value of a person's life is not measured by how much money they've accumulated, how many deals they've done, how many titles they have, but by the quality of their relationships, the impact that they've had on other people's lives, and the willingness and capacity to serve," Givray says. "I believe that if you connect to your values in your decisions and actions, then the other stuff is just the scorecard, and they'll come your way. In 2001, I was going to be out of a job, gave back a million bucks, and like others who had lived through the dot-com bust, I had no significant financial reserves. I certainly had my dreams but I also knew that goals and successes are rarely achieved in a linear fashion. I knew that as long as I found an opportunity where I could continue to grow and learn, and surround myself with people who share my values, I would get there. It might be a zigzag path, but I would get there. Attempting to achieve career milestones based on a prescribed plan at best saps you of productive energy and at worse can result in you missing out on relationships and opportunities that truly matter."

How does Givray's mantra—focus on values—impact his everyday life? He says, "Values guide every aspect of my personal and professional life. How I make decisions, what actions I take, how I interact with people, which type of people I want to hire and work with, how I manage my leadership team, how I communicate, what kind of clients our company will take on, what kind of investors, board members, industry colleagues and service providers I want to interact with. I never focus on building 'credentials' or 'capital'—everything I do must connect to my values and then the accomplishments follow. For me, this makes making decisions and taking action pretty automatic. It's this internal validation checkpoint with my head, heart, and gut. Most of the time it's invisible—you don't even know you're doing it."

"Above all," Givray says, "trust and trustworthiness is the ultimate imperative for success. Developing a network of deep relationships is the most treasured asset that any professional can have. It's all about truly gaining the trust, confidence, credibility, and loyalty of people. It all starts with valuing trust."

He shared these additional personal values: uncompromised integrity; willingness to serve or put service ahead of self; communicating with clarity, frankness and conviction; honoring one's word and delivering on promises and commitments; and finally, courage to always do the right thing, even if it isn't the most popular or expedient course. A person's values are so important that Givray believes that the goal of recruitment is to look for them first. While traditional interviewing methods look at experience level, competency, relevant background, analytical strengths, and job-specific "soft" skills, they often neglect to consider values.

PUTTING VALUES ON THE WALL

Givray's chosen values continued to guide and drive his career as he took his next post, and the rewards to both him and those around him materialized quickly. In 2002, he became CEO of his previous employer, SmithBucklin, the world's largest association management company.

Givray had joined the company in 1983, and four years later he was invited to buy a small ownership stake in the company. At that time, there were a total of 14 owners, some of whom owned more than others. When Givray left SmithBucklin in 1996, four executives owned 80 percent of the company. In 1998, these four sold the company to outside financial investors, who brought in an outside CEO.

"Within two months of selling the legal services company in 2001, I learned that SmithBucklin's financial investors were interested in selling the company," Givray says. "Neither they nor the CEO truly understood SmithBucklin's unique business. Clients, employees and certainly the business and its reputation were suffering. So I called up the financial investors who had recruited me to run the legal services company. I said, 'Are you interested in acquiring SmithBucklin?' They said, 'Only if you come back and run it.' Obviously, I was thrilled to hear that."

One of Givray's very first steps upon his return to SmithBucklin was to help the entire company embrace a well-articulated culture as defined by the company's vision, mission, and chosen values. SmithBucklin's culture is openly communicated and shared. They leave their stated values on the table, or more accurately, the wall, for all to see as they walk in the door of their three offices. Most importantly, everyone throughout the company is truly expected to embrace and internalize them. Givray believes everything starts with articulating an authentic culture that guides and inspires.

"Nurture, protect, and most importantly, live it," he says. "If someone does not live it, they've got to go. Even if you have a star performer who's delivering results, if they're not living the values, they've got to go. As I matured professionally, this principle became one that I was simply not willing to compromise."

Within SmithBucklin, the company's core values guide everyday work and relationships with clients and fellow employees. When asked, Givray readily shares their ten posted values with well thought-out detail and ease. They address issues including client stewardship, people care, passion, customer care, internal cohesiveness and alignment, and of course, trust and trustworthiness. To say he lives, breathes and honors them, would be putting it accurately. It's no surprise that SmithBucklin performance reviews judge employees equally on delivering results and living the company's values.

To understand the power of the SmithBucklin culture and values system, simply consider their real-world business impact. In the four years immediately following Givray's rejoining SmithBucklin, he and his team have shattered every performance record from the previous 50 years—client retention, new client acquisition, employee satisfaction, financial performance—all of them. Happy client organizations saw their goals met, and often exceeded. Client retention was practically 100 percent. Former star employees decided to follow Givray's lead and rejoin the company. The turnaround was astounding—but for Givray, the finest accomplishment was yet to come, and it again involved leaving some money on the table.

TRANSFERRING OWNERSHIP TO EMPLOYEES

In 2005, SmithBucklin transferred ownership from its financial investors to its employees. The day when SmithBucklin's Employee Stock Ownership Plan (ESOP) was finalized became the proudest moment of Henry Givray's entire career.

"Even though I had accomplished my goal of returning to SmithBucklin and leading the company, for me the dream wasn't complete," he says. "The other part of my dream was to be able to offer every SmithBucklin employee, regardless of position or compensation level, an equal opportunity to experience the fulfillment and rewards of ownership."

When pressed, Givray admits that he would most certainly have made more money personally if SmithBucklin had been sold to another set of financial investors rather than to its employees. Doing so, however, would have been inconsistent with his chosen values. Furthermore, the ESOP itself was designed to mirror the culture and values that help the SmithBucklin team excel each day. The ESOP is exceptional for its unique, transparent governance structure and overall design, which allowed every employee a fair and equal opportunity to participate without limitation. The ESOP has added even more horsepower to the values-based engine of SmithBucklin.

Stresses Givray: "Being 100-percent employee-owned means that Joe Jones on the 22nd floor in Chicago is accountable to Jane Smith in DC working in a totally different area. It's shared success, shared responsibility. In most companies, if I work in accounting I may not care about what sales and marketing is doing. But in our case, we're all owners so we're all accountable to each other and care deeply about helping to make one another successful."

Henry Givray gets it. To him, putting values on the wall—and living them—yields impressive, tangible benefits and contributes to both his and his company's ability to be successful. Putting values out there creates loyal and enthusiastic clients, employees, and industry partners. It cultivates a network of deep relationships built and nurtured around trust, respect, confidence, and loyalty. It is not about how much money you get, what deal to negotiate, which title to grab, or which costs to cut. Our seventh step to activate change is all about giving back and giving up to some degree. Put yourself in the middle once in awhile and leave some money on the table. Remember the often-forgotten words of Albert Einstein: "Not everything that can be counted counts, and not everything that counts can be counted."

Jerry Fisher
Retired VP of Corporate R&D at Baxter Healthcare

Leaving Things as Good as They Were Found

With more than 30 years in the health care industry, Jerry Fisher has made a living by caring for others. He has cultivated a commitment to technological innovation while maintaining a focus on the individual patient. Blending technical excellence with personal service is what he tries to convey to those he works with.

Fisher says, "My life's purpose and mission is to leave the world a better place having had me in it. I would like my epitaph to read, 'He cared; he made a difference.'"

He believes leadership is not as much about what you take as it is what you leave behind. Relationships and business transactions have lasting effects on organizations and individuals. If you keep taking and never give anything back, eventually there will not be anything to get.

"I take the approach that you should leave everything you touch as good or better than the way you found it," says Fisher. "My father instilled that in me at a very early age. You can borrow anything on my desk, but I want the desk to look as good as it did when you got it. If we were hunting, we never left anything in the woods that wasn't there when we started. It is a matter of being conscious of not detracting from the value of what is already there and also thinking about what you can do to make it better."

COMMUNICATING TO FIND RESPECT

Fisher grew up with a brother with Down syndrome. It was hard to predict how people would act when they met his brother. Some would patronize him and treat him like a baby. Others would approach him like nothing was unusual. Fisher never knew how it would turn out. His brother, however, knew almost instantaneously whether he was going to like someone or not.

Fisher remembers, "My brother taught me two things. One is that you should respect everybody because they can teach you something very valuable if you just take the effort to notice it. And second, if you want to respect someone, you need to get to know them, and in order to get to know them, you have to communicate."

Leaders need to realize that often the more you are willing to put into a relationship, the more you will get out of it. The easiest and most effective way to gain value in any situation is through communication. Communication builds trust, increases knowledge, and creates shared power. Most importantly, communication signals to others that you are not a threat.

"The people that my brother always took to were the people that treated him like a real person, like a normal person," Fisher says. "They neither talked down to him or over his head. If he was sitting on the floor they sat on the floor, whatever they needed to do, either conversationally or physically. They listened to anything he had to say until he was finished speaking. And I think most importantly of all, they weren't afraid to physically touch him. I very rarely ever saw him not like someone who was worth liking."

AVOIDING THE RATIONALIZATION

Fisher knows that if you think about it long enough, you can convince yourself of anything. A strong set of values "on the table" helps leaders avoid the temptation to over-think.

"There are always opportunities to rationalize a decision that you don't feel good about internally," he says. "That has never worked for me. So I just try to avoid the rationalization and keep things as simple and decisive as possible."

Values are not principles to be called upon only when the decisions are minor or the consequences small. The consistency of values should be the foundation that guides the totality of an organization.

Leaders should embrace values as a way to give them focus in an often-cloudy environment.

"I would like to see people that I call true leaders address the tough issues with the same decisiveness that they make decisions on the easy ones," comments Fisher. "I think that separates true values from pseudo ones about as quickly as anything. When it comes to a life or death situation and it doesn't have a monetary impact, it is an easy decision to make. Can you make that same decision with the same speed, efficiency, directness, and decisiveness if it costs you millions and millions of dollars? To me that's mandatory." When values are in place or "on the table" to guide the decisions, less time is spent on the process of making them, even when they have an impact on the bottom line.

FOLLOWING YOUR HEART ISN'T EASY

During the Vietnam War, several of Fisher's peers volunteered for military service. His closest friend, who was a straight-A medical student with a tremendous future, said, "The world has given so much to me, I have got to give something back." He was killed in action.

Fisher was a pacifist. He believed that saving one life was a bigger contribution to humanity than taking ten. He struggled reconciling his values with his obligation to his country and friends.

"I had to look at myself and ask, 'Why am I doing this?'" Fisher remembers. "Do I really believe in the values of pacifism? I was a pretty aggressive guy. I didn't always live my life so that you could tell I was a pacifist, but that is what I believed. My friends were going and getting killed, why wasn't I willing to do that?"

In the oldest town in West Virginia, Fisher became the first conscientious objector to enroll in the military. He offered to be a medic and go straight to Vietnam. Instead, the Army placed him in a medical testing lab in South Bend, Indiana. During his tour of duty, he developed tests to detect lead poisoning that ended up saving the lives of factory workers.

"In all the coaching and mentoring I do, I try to help people understand why I hold the values that I do," Fisher says. "In putting teams together, I show how mutual respect enhances performance and demonstrate that communication is the way to build that respect. I think that anytime our organization had a program we thought was not going to add value or was not going to make things better, we questioned it, challenged it, and in a lot of cases dropped it. I have taught my groups that if you see something wrong, it is not only okay to question it and put it out in the open, it is mandatory."

PRACTICING THE THREE 'R'S

One of the greatest leaders Fisher ever worked with was former Baxter Healthcare CEO Harry Kraemer. When Kraemer arrived at the company, he provided a clear direction for how decisions would be made. Fisher remembers Kraemer explaining the three 'R's: respect, responsiveness, and results. Kraemer believed that all three should be "on the table" all the time, and the meaning of each value was clearly shared.

Fisher says, "Respect means at every level for every person. Respect means you stand up and be counted. Respect means you don't coward out to somebody else's opinion when you don't believe in it.

"Responsiveness is that we are here to serve the patient. That's who comes first. So anytime you get a call from the outside from a patient, that's your first priority.

"Results mean that if you don't deliver on what you say you are going to deliver, you don't get a chance to do all the fun things we have going on. So if we say we are going to do this right from a financial perspective even though it will have a negative quarterly impact, we are going to do it."

Kraemer wanted everyone to aspire to be a "best partner." Best partners look to create situations where both sides win and are not concerned with trying to cut the best deal at the table.

ENGAGING OTHERS TO GAIN SUPPORT

Fisher was always impressed with Kraemer's hands-on approach to management. His willingness to become personally involved increased the sincerity and strength of his message.

"He took ownership, it was never just someone else's idea," Fisher remembers. "He simplified the ground rules so that everyone understood the values and was engaged. He personally explained each of our principles to everyone in the company either in person or by phone. He said, 'This is why it is important to me; this is why it is important to you; this is why it is important to us.' Everything was put *on the table* in very simple terms in a language anyone could understand."

Great leaders become engaged with those around them. They make goals and expectations clear and create an environment that allows everyone to help the organization reach those ends.

"Kraemer put a few metrics in place and on a monthly basis let us know how we were performing," Fisher says. "He expected success, and he planned for it. He handpicked a leadership team and said, 'These are your role models and if you have any questions, ethically or otherwise, these are the kind of people that I want you to go to and get resolution.' He always made time. I never saw him tell somebody he didn't have time. He listened extremely well and there were absolutely no misinterpretations when you were done with a conversation with Harry."

SUCCESS IS ACHIEVEMENT— FAILURE IS NOT EVEN TRYING

"The minimum level of success is achieving what we say we are going to achieve," Fisher says. "What is true success is when we are able to go above and beyond our set objectives. The more global they are and the greater the impact, then the more you can say you were successful."

To accomplish what you set out do is a deceivingly difficult mission. Leaders must ensure that organizations remain focused on established goals. However, great leaders seize opportunities to reach further and accomplish more.

"To me the biggest failure is not doing something you could have done," Fisher says. "I can rationalize all the other pieces but I can't rationalize not doing something that I knew I could have accomplished." It is no surprise that Fisher's goal is to *always* leave something on the table.

16

Lift People Up

> *"That which seems the height of absurdity in one generation often becomes the height of wisdom in the next."*
> **JOHN STUART MILL**

> *"The development of a model describing how people relate to each other has not evolved yet—but it is the next big step we need to take to make organizations functional."*
> **PAULETTE COLE, CEO of ABC Home in New York**

WHAT IS PEOPLESHIP?

people ('p_-p_l) *n* A group of human beings linked by common interests who share the same values.

ship ('ship) *n* A vehicle designed to operate in free space outside the earth's atmosphere.

peopleship ('p_-p_l 'ship) *n* A new form of leadership that lifts people up, having six qualities and seven culture-changing steps.

Peopleship is a style of leadership that lifts people up. Our six qualities reshape the leadership construct for the future, and change the typical control-and-compete archetype to one that is far more embracing, engaging, and people-oriented. Corporate conference rooms that are currently referred to as "command and control centers" may become far more constructive if called "encourage and enable centers."

Peopleship is a holistic leadership method; if one quality is missing or underdeveloped, it cannot function properly. Humility, compassion, transparency, inclusiveness, collaboration, and values-based decisiveness must work together. The seven steps to change have been created in order to develop these qualities in every individual and organization—not just a few chosen leaders at the top. Employees must also reach out to serve others; ask, "Who am I?"; ask "Who are you?"; find common ground; don't take their pleats out; root for people; and leave some money on the table. There is, then, a lot for everyone to cheer about. Imagine working in a setting where individuals listen deeply, care profoundly, and call forth their maximum potential. Peopleship makes this reality.

A PROFILE OF PEOPLESHIP

It is not a coincidence that the definition of "ship" that we use describes a spacecraft and that the leader profiled in this chapter is an astronaut. Whether high in the sky or on the earth below, Mary Ellen Weber exemplifies our six qualities through her leadership style and insightful messages. For this reason, her leadership profile is shared in detail in our closing chapter. When we began our book, we chose her vignette to introduce the discussion of humility. You may recall the story of how her commander sharing a mistake that he had once made gained him even more respect and helped them all better prepare for their launch. By ending with her profile, she bookends our messages on success and leadership with a synchronicity that seems appropriate.

Think Globally, Act Locally

Mary Ellen Weber
Former NASA astronaut

Mary Ellen Weber understands what it means to have a global perspective, having orbited the earth nearly 300 times. Among the youngest astronauts in the history of NASA, Weber helped construct the International Space Station in 2000, participating in one of the largest cooperative scientific efforts the world has ever seen.

"I really believe in the philosophy, 'Think globally, and act locally,'" says Weber. "You have to decide what you think is important but if you try to change the entire world, it is such a huge mountain that you won't do anything. But if you work on your own, in your own local environment and start by setting an example, even just spreading ideas, it becomes infectious. Eventually it will have a global effect."

EARNING WHAT YOU GET, GETTING WHAT YOU EARN

We live in a goal-oriented society in which results are celebrated without much thought given to how they were achieved. Weber, however, does not believe in hollow victories. Success is fleeting and can be taken away. Pride is permanent.

Weber says, "It is important that you seek to only earn what you deserve and what you work for. I think this is a fundamental change in the mentality of society. It used to be the American dream to work really hard and be a success, and now the American dream is to win the lottery. Now it is more respected to do nothing in your job and get paid a lot than to have worked your way up from the mail room. It is important that you take pride in earning the things that you have and not just looking for ways to get a free lunch."

The business world is full of the dreaded "isms": nepotism, cronyism, favoritism, sexism, and racism. Few things garner resentment and disloyalty among employees more than an arbitrary or subjective reward system.

"You only get what you earn, but it also works the other way in that you need to earn what you get, what you did work for," Weber says. "What I have seen, both personally and from those I have worked with, is that when someone works very hard, when they deliver, it is absolutely devastating if somebody gets the reward for other reasons. It is devastating to the entire culture, and it is devastating to the individuals. I think rewarding people for the work they do, the quality of the work they do and not other more insidious intangible things, that's how you keep loyalty."

As a woman in the male-dominated field of aeronautics, there's no doubt that Weber had to work hard to prove herself. Perhaps this is why judging on the merits of work is so important to her.

ROOTING FOR THOSE AROUND YOU

"I find it very important to root for other people," Weber says. "I think if everybody applied that ideal in their personal and work lives it would be a win-win situation. It can be very tempting to wish that other people fail so that you can succeed. Not only is that bad for them, but personally it detracts from you. And when you root for someone and they succeed, you realize the warm feelings you reap don't take anything away from you. It is tempting to believe that it does, that someone else succeeding takes away from you. You almost have to consciously make sure you don't fall into that trap."

There is a powerful myth that business is inherently competitive. The belief is that there are only so many winners, so every success means one less opportunity for you. Weber realizes that this is a pervasive but flawed mind-set. By viewing yourself as in cooperation and not competition with others, you improve your odds of success while lowering the likelihood of failure. Success is rarely an individual event. The benefits are likely to be shared with those who offered support.

DECIDING TO SUCCEED

"People often talk about success as something that happens to you, but it is a decision," Weber says. "Doing well at something is just a decision. I think it has very little to do with capabilities. I very firmly believe that. Certainly some people are better artists than others, other people can be smarter, but it really is just a decision about how much work you put in and, even more important, what standards you will accept."

Success, believes Weber, is too often viewed as serendipitous. We sit in wonderment, as the same individuals seem to end up on top again and again. Success is not a coincidence; it is the result of preparation, practice, and passion. It is not given, it is learned.

Weber was a baby when her father died. He was a West Point graduate and they had been a military family, moving from base to base and relying on the army. When her father passed away, Weber's mother was left with no job, no college degree, and three small children to care for.

For Weber's mother, it was never a question: All three of her children would go to college. While relying solely on social security and veteran's payments, her mother attended school for six years to become a teacher and better provide for her family. Throughout it all, she made sure her children had dreams and ambitions.

In 2006, Weber's mother died. She had taught for more than 20 years, and shared her work ethic and independent spirit with countless students. Today, her eldest son is a business executive with a PhD and an MBA, her other son has a master's degree in engineering and is a successful attorney, and her daughter holds a PhD, an MBA, and is one of a handful of individuals who has soared amongst the stars.

Weber says, "The values and the way we think about life and the way we go about our business are not something that people are inherently born with. I think they are ideas we are exposed to." She's right. Let's take a look at where the ideas come from.

NORMALIZING EXCELLENCE

"I strive for excellence in the way I work, the way I behave and the way I deal with people," Weber declares. "I think it is very important to do whatever task is ahead of you, and do it very well. And I find that this should not be because you have to; it is important to do it for yourself. It should be out of pride for your own self-worth, for your own self-respect. And it always amazes me when people don't have that value. Whether you are planning a vacation, buying a house, or choosing your friends, it is important that you set really high standards for yourself and that you work towards that."

For great leaders, excellence is not a "sometimes" thing; it is a constant. Weber is not driven by external rewards, she finds fulfillment in the effort toward greatness.

MAXIMIZING YOUR ENERGY OUTPUT

Energy in, energy out. It is a simple equation that guides production. Successful leaders find ways to take personal contributions and create a sum that is greater than anything each individual could have created on their own. Energy cannot be created or destroyed. It can, however, be harnessed, directed, and marshaled to achieve great things.

"Where you place your energy on the individual is in trying to set an example for others," Weber says. "But that ties into putting the energy into the team. You are only one person. The team is many people. If you can contribute to a group of people and if you have 'X' amount of energy to put into making one person's work better or you can put the same amount of energy and improve the work of ten people, obviously it is more important to put that amount of energy in your team."

COAXING OUT EXCELLENCE

Weber says, "I think what you should strive for is to simply put ideas out there that give people food for thought. When Einstein developed his theories, no one had ever considered them before and now people use them every day. The same applies to values and ideas about how we live our lives and what is important. If you put ideas in people's heads, then they will grow."

The International Space Station was the most ambitious and daunting endeavor in the history of NASA. The project was filled with delays and cost overruns. But everyone—from the engineers, to the scientists, to the crew—believed in the mission. Every setback merely increased their resolve. In the end, they were able to create something that will have an immeasurable scientific impact for decades to come.

Weber says, "I think a skill that is underdeveloped is how you get the best from other people, how you inspire them to deliver a kind of excellence—not just for your needs, but for their own personal reward. I think when people do experience working hard at something and having it come out well, and being recognized for it, that in and of itself tends to be great motivation for people to do that in the future. But many people never really experience that. It takes a great leader to coax them through all of that."

Every day we are reminded of our shortcomings. There is always another rung to climb, or another ceiling to break through. Weber thinks less about challenges and more in terms of opportunities. Great leaders convey the inherent value of effort. They set an example for excellence and motivate others to join them.

LIVING UP TO GOOD (AND BAD) EXPECTATIONS

Life is in many ways a self-fulfilling prophecy. We see ourselves the way we are seen by others.

"I think we very much live up to expectations that people place on us, both the good and the bad," Weber says. "The more we categorize people or pin traits on them, the more they tend to live up to those things. I make a conscious effort not to categorize things."

Stereotypes are easy. They let leaders act toward people in prescribed, predetermined ways. However, Weber prefers to let people define themselves by their actions. She asks for excellence, roots for success for everyone, and in doing so allows individuals around her to grow.

THE FUTURE WORKPLACE

Let's jump ahead to the year 2020. Meet Steve Forte, an administrative assistant who works with Henry Parsons, the executive director of a not-for-profit organization. Steve has been associated with his "boss" for six years now, since 2014, and they have developed a warm, caring, and enriching professional relationship with each other. Steve has an intuitive sense and bond with Henry that often enables him to anticipate Henry's requests and virtually finish sentences and thoughts before Henry completes them.

Steve and Henry trust each other. They work together well. They have two fundamental principles in place: Always be open and honest with each other, and respect each other's individuality. This simple "norm and value statement" between them has provided a strong relationship. This has enabled the two of them to flourish. Henry has been on a "fast track," and Steve has really helped to further accelerate Henry's career. Steve gets personal satisfaction from that.

Even though Steve plays a "behind-the-scenes" job function, he has always felt great about his job. That's because Henry has consistently made Steve feel an integral part of the team. Steve has become his trusted adviser and confidant as well as his professional friend.

Steve would describe his job to other friends in this way: "For as long as I can remember, Henry has always treated me with kindness, respect, and consideration. He expresses appreciation almost daily for my initiatives and gives me praise often. He makes me feel good about myself. Just being near him provides me with an inner sense of self-confidence. It's hard to explain—Henry just really knows me and understands me."

LOOKING FORWARD AND LAUNCHING PEOPLESHIP

Like in the example of Steve and Henry, effective leaders possess the ability to get the most out of the individuals they work with. They understand that cultivating the talents of those around them is one of the most powerful ways to move an organization forward.

In the future workplace, managers as we know them today will disappear. The title "manager" suggests that one person is superior, the other subordinate. This archaic approach will vanish when employees and leaders learn to work side-by-side as equal partners—achieving an organization's goals together. Frankly, managers are often the "bad guys" in our typical work organizations. They have *no* inner, emotionally charged, intuitive energy. When they act, they tend to pit themselves against employees in a managers-versus-employees game. When this occurs, managers do not view employees as important.

What must happen in the workplace? Employees need to know that a leader cares for them and is there for them—just as children need to know this from their parents. As a leader, being available and responsive is the most important job. Child psychologists use the phrase "good enough parent." It means that a parent does not have to be brilliant, funny, good in sports, rich, or blessed with many talents. Rather, a parent needs to *be there*—emotionally and physically—so that the child experiences his or her love. This is a "good enough parent." Similarly, a "good enough leader" is emotionally and physically available, not distant, and unresponsive.

When employees become attached to a leader, that employee is a stronger, more participative member of the workplace. Ironically, "becoming attached" creates employees who are more secure, independent, and liberated thinkers. They are lifted up. Unattached employees spend their time trying to play politics and are haunted by the insecurities of organizational hierarchy. They are *not* lifted up.

What can leaders do to activate the peopleship model? Organizations must be built on change and flexibility, not rigidity. Autocratic and hierarchical organizations need to be radically modified. We encourage a new way of organizing the workplace. It is a form of shared leadership called "peopleship." It is a construct with no hierarchy, where people are treated and act as equals, even though their jobs are totally different. Our shared leadership construct focuses on the essential spirit or bond that can occur among any "crew." Each crewmember is equal in value to the others. When organizations nurture this equality, each member feels important because they are. Each has equal significance within the group. This does not assume that all members have the same skills or equal gifts. There are major differences among each other's strengths, but each person has unique talents that contribute to the group. Interactions are guided by humility, compassion, transparency, inclusiveness, collaboration, and values-based decisiveness.

To launch the peopleship process, let's reach out to serve others. Let's ask: Who am I? And who are you? Let's find common ground. Let's not take out our pleats. Let's root for each other. Let's leave some money on our table. Then, we can be lifted up. Six, five, four, three, two, one. Blast off!

Epilogue:
The Peopleship Planet

"Life's tragedy is that we get old too soon and wise too late."
BEN FRANKLIN

We believe the planet can change. Our hope is that we will not, in the words of Ben Franklin, become "wise too late." If people embrace our six leadership qualities and activate our seven steps to change, a peopleship organization can emerge. How long will the transition take? Most likely, it will require decades. But we can change the stereotypes and behaviors that have defined success in the past.

Success should be defined as a combination of empowering the self while at the same time serving others. This definition dispels the myth that leaders at the top need to control and compete to be effective and successful. Our 25 leaders represent a new model for the future, one that says there are effective ways to manage organizations and make profits without leaving a sense of humanity at the office door.

In a time when fallen leaders and the organizations they have destroyed litter the news, *Apples Are Square* is a book that focuses on success. We have shared the ideas, experience, and values of 25 people who are leading the way to a new definition of leadership in the early 21st century.

Six uncommon—but very human—qualities guide our model: humility, compassion, transparency, inclusiveness, collaboration, and values-based decisiveness. It comes as no surprise then that the model for change that emerges is called "peopleship." The "peopleship" approach cultivates multiple leaders in an organization. It strengthens individuals, enabling them to be recognized and valued.

It connects employees and managers in building strong relationships. Those who embrace the "peopleship" model will learn important new ways to strengthen their organization's culture while rebuilding and renewing faith in the workplace.

Contrary to the old model for success, which was derived from money, control, power, and ego, there is a new model for greatness. It is humility. It becomes the cornerstone of leadership. The stereotypical male ego, in particular, seems to fight this idea. Many individuals are unwilling to visibly show any vulnerabilities or insecurities. As a result, they hide their real feelings and are often perceived as arrogant. Long ago, the original idea of the sacred king was that he was the *servant* of the land. He served the people, and he was both noble and full of humility. Today, leadership again requires a humble focus on service. The leaders with whom we spoke shared a common sentiment: the greater the humility, the greater magnetism of that leader to the people within his or her organization.

Our new leadership model asks you to contribute your total self, to convey empathy, and to show you really care. It requires that you add texture to your relationships so that employees and managers bond. Moreover, it encourages you to show personal warmth, pulling others in by being a good listener and asking questions. This type of emotional communication builds a "culture of caring" within the organization in which people can flourish. Success, then, is defined by helping others. Ask yourself: "Did I make them feel better about themselves? Did I make them feel like they were capable of achieving more than they ever thought they could?"

Transparency is the attribute of a culture within an organization where there is openness, sharing of information, fairness, and a sense of integrity. One of the leaders who spoke with us emphasized: Outcome or result is the "sight," and the process to reach the outcome is the "insight." If the process is transparent, then insights are received. Transparency is about opening up and being accessible and in touch with one's self to create an environment of trust and candidness. It deals with sharing and communicating data, perspectives, observations, and viewpoints—both good and bad. It's about letting people make choices and their own decisions.

People need to have a voice. Leaders need to accept the differences in people and make them feel included and valued. In any environment, they have to feel part of the decision-making process. At work, employees should feel that a decision was not a one-person pronouncement. There must be opportunities for employees to contribute their inputs and to hear the voices of others. Most importantly, people need to know that their comments are heard and their contributions are valued. This creates a culture of inclusiveness.

Working together as a team rather than competing with each other enables better problem-solving and decision-making to occur. The worst leader is someone who chooses to use people for personal gain, rather than champion employee advancement or confidence. The outdated leadership mind-set sees people or workers as a resource for consumption. Its leaders are interested in acquiring or maintaining power. They believe: I have the power, because you don't. If others become self-empowered, then I lose power. It's either them or me. In this culture, collaboration does not exist. Self-respect and self-empowerment also run out the door. Creating a spirit of collaboration is all about instilling an ongoing mind-set where people intrinsically want to work together to help both the individual and the group succeed. There is partnership.

Given the countless decisions that must be made, individuals often avoid putting a stake in the ground to make a clear-cut decision. Or worse, leaders don't make a decision. However, when values lead the decision-making process, it is effortless. Decisiveness means putting values at the top of mind as one makes a decision. Values act as a filter or compass in the decision-making process. Values-based thinking can and should guide all decisions within a group or organization.

Our six leadership qualities and seven steps work hand-in-hand with each other. While you may not be able to activate all seven steps in your organization, each one that is undertaken will further advance the peopleship mind-set. We summarize the steps as follows:

- *Reach Out to Serve Others*—Start with an other-directed mind-set and a service orientation. The first step is to reach out, beyond one's self and one's organization. Connect with the rest of society and the wider world. Commitment to social causes is essential. Whether helping to save the environment, mitigating poverty, improving education, or increasing respect for women in developing countries—serving others benefits and bridges individuals and organizations. Reaching out and doing something to help others is a universal responsibility. Each of us of can serve. It is a job that should not be delegated to others or brushed away. Giving magnifies our hearts in a way that loosens us up to better communicate, interact, and understand others.

- *Ask, "Who Am I?"*—We must each get to know our personal values, needs, strengths, weaknesses, and the factors that have shaped our values. When we address the question, "Who am I?" we discover our inner treasure. Knowing who you are can help to identify activities for personal growth. What do you want to achieve, learn, acquire, and master in the workplace? How can you find ways to achieve your personal goals? The work culture should value more than just bottom-line growth and security. It must be a pathway to personal discovery. Organizations need to first focus on the individual.

- *Ask, "Who Are You?"*—While individuals in a group must give attention to their own needs and interests, they must also interact with other group members and help them address their needs and interest. Leaders need to spend lots of time with employees communicating, mentoring, and coaching. There is nothing more important than building, maintaining and perpetuating relationships, and helping others grow to reach their maximum potential. This is what a leader must do. Passion, compassion, exhilaration, and even laughter can enrich relationships. Direct, deep, open, two-way talk is the key. The new mantra is get to know the strengths of others, help them experience personal success, use descriptive praise to motivate and facilitate personal growth, and give advice on how to improve. Create a "helping community" to support each other, call forth their inner talents, and be present and available to others in their group.

- *Find Common Ground*—Once a leader has an understanding of the individual, then that leader is able to build relationships connecting individuals. Culture is an amalgam of individuals, who share a common goal. Everyone within an organization needs to play a vital, supportive, and interconnected role. The best model for effective learning is a small, sharing group. "Deep listening" is nurtured among group members. Carol Bernick, chairman of the board of Alberto-Culver, believes in helping people find each other's connecting points. She sums it up this way: "I don't go around saying 'I'm going to be one of Fortune's most powerful women.' That just doesn't really interest me. I really have always just wanted to be in an organization where I made a difference and where I was working with a great group of people that I really enjoyed who were making a difference."

- *Don't Take the Pleats Out*—A key challenge for leadership is to "not take the pleats out." This means let individuals flourish. Be emotive. Let passion and creativity reign. Employees must experience the freedom to pursue their unique interests, desires, enthusiasms, knowledge, and skills. They must be able to apply them to numerous opportunities and problems within the workplace. Work becomes an act of creative professional expression. A professional purity exists because the culture is not prohibitive. Individuals can work at full capacity. Creative fire and professional passion thrive. Everyone has a unique genius within; our new people approach lets it out.

- *Root for People*—This new approach places thought and focus on encouraging people around us, not the leaders at the top. When we support, promote, and root for others, then it is a win-win situation for everybody. Consequently, we find people far more able and willing to see leaders as facilitators, as peers, and as equals at work. Everyone listens deeply and cares profoundly. A powerful transformation occurs. Rather than follow a leader, the people now root for others.

- *Leave Some Money on the Table*—Negotiating for the last cent or jockeying for the best position or project does not always yield the greatest results in the long run. It sounds like it would—always trying to optimize—but other people will feel squeezed or suboptimized after awhile. They just will not feel equal or that a mutual respect exists. Instead, a sense will emerge that gain will come at their expense—a situation that will not continue long. What is better is to leave some money on the table. Moreover, when you are making decisions and taking action, you should *always* bring values to that table. Choosing the financially beneficial or expedient short-term path is not always the best move.

"Peopleship" is a new form of leadership that lifts people up. The "ship" of "peopleship" is a vehicle designed to operate in space—outside the earth's atmosphere. Hence, the atmosphere or culture of the workplace must nurture a sense of freedom, and the people within must be given more attention. Let's lift them up and launch peopleship at work. Together, we can create a peopleship planet. Together, we can change the way we lead and succeed.

Index

A

Accountability, 59, 192
Adaptability, 64–65
Anton, Susan
  on family, 120–21
  on inclusiveness, 118–19
  on loyalty, 119–20
  profile, 118
  success metrics, 122–23
  on teamwork, 123–24
Authenticity, 46

B

Bernick, Carol
  collaboration, 90–95
  deep listening, 229
  personal failures, 94
  personal success, 91–92
  profile, 90
Buffet, Warren, 9
Business transparency, 54–55

C

Caring attitude, 27–28, 30, 226
Chambers, John, 79–80
Cisco Systems, 79–80
Clayton, Galeta
  core values, 99
  profile, 99
  value-based decisiveness, 100–106
  values, 97–98
Cohen, Leonard, 78
Colbert, Steven, 78
Cole, Paulette, 124–25

Collaboration
  achieving, 93–95
  definition of, 20, 84–85
  importance of, 227
  keys to, 86–89
  practicing, 90–93
Command-and-control, 187–88
Commitment, 228
Common ground, 157–71, 229
Communication
  expressive, 180–83
  interpersonal, 87
  new ways of, 5
  power of, 90–91
  respect through, 208–10
  value of, 43
Community, 166–67
Compassion
  acts of, 38–40
  benefits of, 39–41
  definition of, 19, 36–37
  manifesting, 37–38
  practicing, 41–51
  root of, 35–36
  sharing, 50
Compassionate listening, 41–43
Compassionate talking, 43–44
Competitive mindset, 100–101
Complacency, 198–99
Compromise, 20, 103–4
Conflict events, 143
Constructive criticism, 154–55
Constructively vulnerable, 29–30
Corporate culture, 205–6
Courage, 133
Creativity, 173–75, 229

Critics, 122
Cultural issues, 167
Culture, 21–22, 229
Customer service, 75–76

D

Decision-making, 21, 98–111
Deep listening, 49, 229
Delay, Tom, 6
Depersonalization, 137–38
Descriptive praise, 153–54
Despres, Leon, 177–79
Determination, 170
Dewey, John, 43
Dictatorial mindset, 95
Disengagement, 169
Diversity, 17–18
Diversity programs, 69
Domino effect, 196–97
Dutton, Jane, 40
Dysfunctional management, 7

E

Ebbers, Bernard, 6
Egocentric leaders, 6
Eisley, Loren, 38–39
Emotional connection, 92–93
Empathy, 12, 50, 226
Empowerment, 88
Encouragement, 194–200, 229–30
Energy, 220
Ensemble, 85–86
Entitlement, 20
Excellence, 220, 221
Exclusion, 68
Expectations, 221–22

F

Facilitate-and-cheer, 188
Failure, 151, 162–63
Family, 120–21
Family values, 135
Feuerstein, Aaron, 41
Fisher, Jerry
    collaboration, 84–85
    on failure, 212–13
    on humility, 210–11
    on individual, 145–46
    rationalization, 209–10
    on respect, 208–9
    success model, 13–14
Fitzgerald, Patrick, 78
Forward momentum, 168
Frost, Peter, 40

G

Gates, Bill, 7, 9
Gilman, Robin, 180–83
Gilmore, Virginia Duncan
    compassionate life, 46–49
    compassion, 50–51
    empathy, 49–50
    humility, 18–19
    learning, 49
    values, 47–48
Giving mindset, 117
Givray, Henry, 202–7
Golden Rule, 107–8
Governmental transparency, 55
Greed, 9
Greenberg, Hank, 6, 10

H

Haley, Alex, 195
Hall, Joel
    adaptability, 64–65
    mindset, 65
    profile, 61–62
    self-respect, 63–64
    transparency, 61–63
Hierarchical system, 70
History, 72–73, 195
Hitsh, Abel, 178
Hoffer, Kaethe Morris, 146–49
Holtz, Lou, 15, 83–84
Human advantage, 10
Human development, 150–51
Humility
    action plan, 32–33
    benefit of, 27–28
    definition of, 18–19, 26
    importance of, 226
    inclusiveness and, 69
    inner, 28–31
    practice, 31–32

precedent for, 25–26
service orientation and, 121

I

Imagination, 197
Inclusiveness
  creation of, 71–74
  definition of, 20, 68
  organizational, 79–81
  practicing, 74–79
  reason for, 70–71
  requisite for, 68
  service orientation and, 118–22
Individual transparency, 55
Inner core, 4
Inner strengths, 73
Innovation, 159, 184–86
Insignificance, 26, 28–29
Integrity, 53–54
Intervention, 149
Intuition, 174

J

Jain, Dipak
  decision-making, 201
  on hierarchical system, 28
  humility, 33
  inclusiveness, 67–74
  profile, 69
  value structure, 72
Jennings, Kevin Melville
  family values, 135
  loyalty, 137
  profile, 132
  self-realization, 133–34, 138–43
  shame, 135–36
  values, 133

K

Kamen, Dean
  challenging values, 163–64
  on failure, 162–63
  innovation and risk, 159
  profile, 160
  on team, 161–62
  valuing vs managing, 164–65
Keating, Thomas, 40–41

Kindness, 117, 147–49
Kozlowski, Dennis, 6
Kraemer, Harry, 211, 212

L

Lafley, A.G., 8
Larrimore, Randy
  compassion, 35–36, 38–39
  personal values, 107–11
  profile, 106–7
Laughter, 44
Law, Cardinal Bernard, 6
Leader
  compassionate, 36
  egocentric, 6
  future traits, 4–5
  humanness of, 12
  passion of, 13–14
  past traits, 4
  role of, 7
Leadership
  emotional depth, 11
  human side of, 10
  qualities, 18–21, 22–23
Learning, 49, 142–43
Lewis, Charles
  profile, 56, 57
  success model, 32
  transparency crusade, 58–61
Life changes, 142–43
Listening
  compassionate, 41–43
  deep, 49, 229
  flexibility and, 181
Loyalty
  demise, 7
  fostering, 11–12, 136–37
  money and, 119–20
Lutz, Scott, 176, 183–86

M

Mackey, John, 80–81
Malden Mills, 41
Merit-based rewards, 217–18
Mindset, 22–23, 65
Mistakes, 94–95, 139
Motivation, 4, 153–54
Mutual relationships, 89

N

Needs, 140, 152
Newmark, Craig
  life lesson, 78–79
  personal values, 76–77
  professional mission, 77–79
  profile, 75–76

O

Organizational inclusiveness, 79–81
Organizational transparency, 60–61
Organizational values, 104–7
Orientation, 4
Other-realization, 40–41, 145–55, 228

P

Palmisano, Samuel, 55–56
Passion, 13–14, 167–68, 229
Patton, Vincent, 188–89, 194–200
People, 7–8
Peopleship, 5
  definition of, 215–16, 230
  leadership qualities, 225–27
  profile of, 216–22
  steps, 228–30
  workplace, 222–24
Perfection, 88–89
Personal characteristics, 140
Personal failures, 94
Personal relationships, 142
Personal success, 153
Personal values
  discovering, 228
  shaping of, 142–43
  understanding, 139–40
Personal zone, 27
Political correctness, 103–4
Positive attitude, 3–4
Potential, 105
Pride, 93–94
Proactive advice, 154–55
Professional passion, 175–86
Propaganda, 57, 58–59

R

Rationalization, 209–10
Rechelbacher, Horst, 128
Recognition, 39, 44–46
Relationships, 228–29
Respect
  attention versus, 47–48
  communicating, 208–9
  other-realization and, 148–49
  requiremetns of, 101
Responsiveness, 211
Results, 186, 211
Rewards, 217–18
Rigas, John, 6
Riopelle, Jack, 12
  business trasparency, 55
  connections with others, 152–55
  on failure, 151
  human development, 150–51
  humility, 30–31
  integrity, 53–54
  success metrics, 150
Risk-aversion, 159

S

Schakowsky, Jan, 188–93
Scrushy, Richard, 6
Self-confidence, 28–29, 63–64
Self-discovery, 40–41
Self-esteem, 29
Selfishness, 198
Self-realization, 132–43
Self-respect, 63–64
Self-worth, 5
Senior, Kimberly, 85–89
Servant mindset, 9
Service orientation
  humility and, 121
  loyalty, 119–20
  meeting needs, 118–19
  other-realization and, 228
  reason for, 116–17
  results of, 115–16
  social change and, 127–28
  transparency and, 126–27
Shame, 135–36
Sinegal, Jim, 7
Skilling, Jeffrey, 6
Social causes, 228
Sorge, Brian
  common ground, 157–58, 166–71

community, 166–67
cultural issues, 167
disengagement, 169
forward momentum, 168
passion, 167–68
profile, 165–66
Standards, 15–16
Star Thrower, The, 38–39
Stereotypes, 222
Stewart, Jon, 78
Stone, W. Clement, 175
Stonecipher, Harry, 6
Strengths/weaknesses, 140–41
Success
    definition of, 225
    metrics, 13–18, 122–23
    new definition of, 4
    '90s benchmark for, 5
    redefinition of, 9–10
    self-centered standard for, 5–6

T

Team, 161–62
Teamwork, 102–3, 124–24
Transparency
    adaptability and, 64–65
    benefits of, 54, 56–61
    definition of, 19, 54
    focus on, 59–60
    importance of, 226–27
    loving mindset and, 65
    practicing, 61–65
    self-respect and, 63–64
    service orientation and, 126–27
    types of, 54–56

U

Unconditional love, 65

V

Value, 139
Value-based decisiveness
    benefits of, 101–4
    definition of, 21, 98–101
    practicing, 104–11
    importance of, 227

Values
    challenges, 109–10, 163–64
    co-creating, 126–27
    consistency of, 209–10
    focus on, 203–5
    passion and, 167–68
    philosophy, 92
    in relationships, 108–9
    reliance on, 185
    teamwork and, 102–3
    through action, 4
    transparency of, 55–56
Vocational diversity, 198–99
Vulnerability, 29–30, 46, 88–89

W

Weber, Mary Ellen
    on humility, 25–26
    profile, 217
    recognition, 39
    reward systems, 217–18
    on success, 218–22
Whitman, May, 8
Whole Foods Market, 80–81
Win-win scenario, 71–72

Z

Zorich, Chris
    anecdote, 3–4
    collaboration, 83–84
    compassion, 37–38
    profile, 14–15
    standards, 15–16
    success metrics, 15–18
    success model, 8
Zorich, Zora, 14–15